INSIGHT FOR LIV
INSIGHTS AND APP

DANIEL

Volume 2

GOD'S PLAN for the FUTURE

FROM THE BIBLE-TEACHING MINISTRY OF

CHARLES R. SWINDOLL

INSIGHT FOR LIVING

DANIEL, VOLUME 2
God's Plan for the Future

From the Bible-Teaching ministry of Charles R. Swindoll

Charles R. Swindoll has devoted his life to the clear, practical teaching and application of God's Word and His grace. A pastor at heart, Chuck has served as senior pastor to congregations in Texas, Massachusetts, and California. He currently pastors Stonebriar Community Church in Frisco, Texas, but Chuck's listening audience extends far beyond a local church body. As a leading program in Christian broadcasting, *Insight for Living* airs in major Christian radio markets around the world, reaching people groups in languages they can understand. Chuck's extensive writing ministry has also served the body of Christ worldwide and his leadership as president and now chancellor of Dallas Theological Seminary has helped prepare and equip a new generation for ministry. Chuck and Cynthia, his partner in life and ministry, have four grown children and ten grandchildren.

In 2008 the original Daniel series was divided into two smaller series. The first volume was subtitled *God's Man for the Moment*. The second volume was subtitled *God's Plan for the Future*. Based upon the original outlines, charts, and transcripts of Charles R. Swindoll's sermons, the Bible Companion text was written by Derrick G. Jeter, Th.M., Dallas Theological Seminary, a writer in the Creative Ministries Department of Insight for Living.

Based upon the original outlines, charts, and transcripts of Charles R. Swindoll's sermons, in 1996, the study guide was developed and written by Bryce Klabunde, a graduate of Biola University and Dallas Theological Seminary.

Published By:
IFL Publishing House
A Division of Insight for Living
Post Office Box 251007
Plano, Texas 75025-1007

Editor in Chief: Cynthia Swindoll, President, Insight for Living
Executive Vice President: Wayne Stiles, Th.M., D.Min., Dallas Theological Seminary
Theological Editor: Brianna Barrier Engeler, M.A., Biblical Studies, Dallas Theological Seminary
Content Editor: Amy L. Snedaker, B.A., English, Rhodes College
Copy Editors: Jim Craft, M.A., English, Mississippi College
Melanie Munnell, M.A., Humanities, The University of Texas at Dallas
Project Coordinator, Creative Ministries: Kim Gibbs, Trinity Valley Community College, 1991–1993
Project Coordinator, Communications: Karen Berard, B.A., Mass Communications,
Texas State University-San Marcos
Proofreader: Paula McCoy, B.A., English, Texas A&M University-Commerce
Cover Designer: Amarilys Henderson, B.F.A., Illustration, Savannah College of Art and Design
Production Artist: Nancy Gustine, B.F.A., Advertising Art, University of North Texas
Cover Image: Copyright © 2008 Jupiterimages Corporation

ISBN: 978-1-57972-817-5
Printed in the United States of America

TABLE OF CONTENTS

A LETTER FROM CHUCK

Winston Churchill knew how to turn a phrase. In a 1939 radio address, he described Russia's actions at the start of World War II as "a riddle wrapped in a mystery inside an enigma."[1] Churchill's words could also apply to the visions and prophecies of Daniel.

The book of Daniel has the unusual distinction of being one of the most well-known—but least-understood—books in the Bible. Most folks are probably familiar with the first half of the book—the accounts of Shadrach, Meshach, and Abed-nego in the fiery furnace, of Daniel in the lions' den, and of the floating hand writing on the wall. But on the other hand, the chapters that record Daniel's visions and prophecies are some of the most enigmatic and mysterious words in all of Scripture.

Many readers of Daniel, theologians and Bible teachers included, avoid the prophetic portions. Even Daniel confessed, in a verse that always makes me grin when I read it, "I heard but could not understand" (Daniel 12:8). My thinking is this: If Daniel—who heard it straight from the angel's mouth—scratched his head in puzzlement, we're in good company!

Now, wait a moment. Before you decide to slam this book shut, believing that Daniel's visions are hopelessly complicated, please—let me offer you a word of encouragement. You *can* begin to understand these prophecies and their impact on your life. That's why we at Insight for Living have written *Daniel, Volume 2: God's Plan for the Future Bible Companion*—to help you unwrap the mystery and apply its life-changing truths. God didn't direct Daniel to record these prophecies to confuse us! God gave them and preserves them for us to study and learn what He has planned for the future. And once we grasp God's purpose, we'll also confess with Daniel:

> "Blessed be the name of God,
> forever and ever.
> He knows all, does all:
> He changes the seasons and guides history."
> (Daniel 2:20–21 MSG)

Charles R. Swindoll

HOW TO USE THIS BIBLE COMPANION

The book of Daniel, like the book of Revelation, has intrigued readers and students for years. Its prophecies and visions are some of the most difficult to interpret in all of Scripture. But because they are so far-reaching and recorded in such vivid detail, understanding the prophecies of Daniel becomes the key to understanding all other biblical prophecy.

Divided into two sections, the first six chapters of the book of Daniel are narrative in form and contain some of the most recognizable stories in the Bible. (You can study the first six chapters in *Daniel, Volume 1: God's Man for the Moment Bible Companion.*) The last six chapters are filled with visions of future events. Everything chronicled in these chapters was future to Daniel. Most of it is history to us now . . . but not all. In this Bible Companion, *Daniel, Volume 2: God's Plan for the Future*, we'll explore Daniel's visions and the prophecies given to him by the angel Gabriel, learning that God reigns as sovereign over the past, the present, and the future.

You may choose to work through this Bible Companion individually or with a group, but regardless of how you choose to complete this study, a brief introduction to the overall structure of each lesson will help you get the most out of it.

LESSON ORGANIZATION

THE HEART OF THE MATTER highlights the main idea of each lesson for rapid orientation. The lesson itself is then composed of two main teaching sections for insight and application:

DISCOVERING THE WAY explores the principles of Scripture through observation and interpretation of the Bible passages, drawing out practical principles for life. Parallel passages and additional questions supplement the main Scriptures for a more in-depth study.

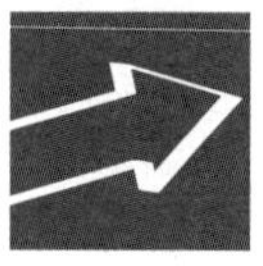

STARTING YOUR JOURNEY focuses on application, helping you to put into practice the principles of the lesson in ways that fit your personality, gifts, and level of spiritual maturity.

USING THE BIBLE COMPANION

Daniel, Volume 2: God's Plan for the Future Bible Companion is designed with individual study in mind, but it may be adapted for group study. If you choose to use this Bible Companion in a group setting, please keep in mind that many of the lessons ask personal, probing questions, seeking to elicit answers that reveal an individual's true character and challenge the reader to change. Therefore, the answers to some of the questions in this Bible Companion may be potentially embarrassing if they are shared in a group setting. Care, therefore, should be taken by the group leader to prepare the group for the sensitive nature of these studies, to forgo certain questions if they appear to be too personal, and to remain perceptive to the mood and dynamics of the group if questions or answers become uncomfortable.

Whether you use this Bible Companion in groups or individually, we recommend the following method:

Prayer—Begin each lesson with prayer, asking God to teach you through His Word and to open your heart to the self-discovery afforded by the questions and text of the lesson.

Scripture—Have your Bible handy. We recommend the New American Standard Bible or another literal translation, rather than a paraphrase. As you progress through each lesson, you'll be prompted to read relevant sections of Scripture and answer questions related to the topic. You will also want to look up the Scripture passages noted in parentheses.

Questions—As you encounter the questions, approach them wisely and creatively. Not every question will be applicable to each person all the time. Use the questions as general guides in your thinking rather than rigid forms to complete. If there are things you just don't understand or that you want to explore further, be sure to jot down your thoughts or questions.

SPECIAL BIBLE COMPANION FEATURES

Throughout the chapters, you'll find several special features designed to add insight or depth to your study. Use these features to enhance your study and deepen your knowledge of Scripture, history, and theology:

GETTING TO THE ROOT

While our English versions of the Scriptures are reliable, studying the original languages can often bring to light nuances of the text that are sometimes missed in translation. This feature explores the meaning of the underlying Hebrew or Greek words or phrases in a particular passage, sometimes providing parallel examples to illuminate the meaning of the inspired biblical text.

DIGGING DEEPER

Various passages in Scripture touch on deeper theological or prophetic questions. This feature will help you gain deeper insight into specific theological issues related to the biblical text.

DOORWAY TO HISTORY

Sometimes the chronological gap that separates us from the original author and readers clouds our understanding of a passage of Scripture. This feature takes you back in time to explore the surrounding history, culture, and customs of the ancient world.

Our prayer is that this Insight for Living Bible Companion will not only help you to dig deeper into God's Word but also provide insights and application for *real* life.

GOD'S PLAN *for the* FUTURE

DANIEL

AUTHOR: DANIEL — DATE: SIXTH-CENTURY BC

	Biographical Section Daniel Interprets Others' Dreams MAIN EMPHASIS: DANIEL THE PROPHET **Outline** Chapter 1: Introduction and Setting Chapter 2: Nebuchadnezzar's Major Dream Chapters 3–6: Historical Narratives (political and personal) *CHAPTERS 1–6*		Prophetic Section Angel Interprets Daniel's Dream MAIN EMPHASIS: THE PROPHECIES OF DANIEL **Outline** Chapter 7: Daniel's Major Vision Chapters 8–12: Prophetic Visions (near and far) *CHAPTERS 7–12*	
Political Powers in Daniel's Day and Afterward	Babylon (605–539 BC) Nebuchadnezzar Belshazzar	Medo-Persia (539–331 BC) Darius (Mede) Cyrus (Persian)	Greece (331–63 BC) Alexander the Great Four Generals	Rome (63 BC–AD 70) Republic and Empire Western Nations (tribulation)
Key Verse	"The Most High is ruler over the realm of mankind." (Daniel 4:17; 5:21)			
Illustration of Christ	The Rock (Daniel 2:34–35); The Son of Man (Daniel 7:13–14); The Messiah Cut Off (Daniel 9:25–26)			
Purpose	God is sovereign over the affairs of humanity and rules the nations according to His will.			

LESSON ONE

A PROPHETIC COLLAGE

Daniel 7

THE HEART OF THE MATTER

As we turn the page from chapter 6 to 7 in the book of Daniel, we leave the relatively simple narrative and biographical sections to enter more difficult and mysterious portions of prophecy.

Through seemingly random and disjointed images, Daniel 7 offers an overview of God's grand design for humanity—all of which was future to Daniel, but some of which is past history to us. In this collage of prophecy, we'll see the sovereignty of God once again and remember that we can trust in Him, both for today and tomorrow.

DISCOVERING THE WAY

Many view biblical prophecy as simply unbelievable. Instead, they take seriously Winston Churchill's tongue-in-cheek comment: "I always avoid prophesying beforehand, because it is a much better policy to prophesy after the event has already taken place."[1] However, history has borne out Daniel's prophecies as "history written beforehand."[2] And to deny this truth is to deny the very sovereignty of God that gives us hope for the present and future.

DIGGING DEEPER
The Purpose of Prophecy

As we embark upon the study of prophecy in the book of Daniel, we would do well to remember two vital truths. First, the Bible is God's inerrant Word, a reliable map for the present as well as the future. No matter how difficult it is to comprehend the mind-blowing visions recorded by Daniel, we must not forget that God has chosen to give us a glimpse of what lies ahead. As we come to understand the big picture of God's perfect, ultimate plan, we need not be disturbed or confused by those details that remain a mystery.

Second, God's sovereignty replaces fear with hope. People all over the world live under superstition, fear of the unknown, apprehension about the future, and an overwhelming feeling that the world is out of control. However, the prophecy contained in His Word shows that God is constantly working out His sovereign purposes. Knowledge of this fundamental truth should help us replace fear with hope and confidence.

In the box, write down all of the many words or phrases that spring to your mind when you think about prophecy, God's sovereignty, the present, and the future.

AN OVERVIEW OF DANIEL 7

A collage is a piece of art created from an array of images, pictures, words, and drawings. When we look at it piece-by-piece or bit-by-bit, it is almost impossible to interpret the artist's statement or purpose. But when we step back and view the whole, suddenly the collage takes on new meaning. The prophecies given to Daniel are much like a collage. If we look at each small part alone, God's message is hard to understand. But when we see the book as a whole and place it within the context of the rest of Scripture, the pieces come together to create a coherent picture. To begin, let's establish the outline of Daniel 7—chronologically, structurally, and comparatively.

Read Daniel 7:1.

Chronologically, Daniel chapter 7 fits between chapters 4 and 5—between Nebuchadnezzar's humiliation and restoration and Belshazzar's fall. The first year of Belshazzar's coregency was probably 553 BC.[3] Most historians believe that Nabonidus, Belshazzar's father, served three years as sole monarch, beginning in 556 BC, before naming his son as coregent. Daniel's first vision, then, occurred about fourteen years before Babylon fell to the Medo-Persians (539 BC). He was approximately 68 years old at the time.[4]

Structurally, Daniel's vision is divided into four sections. The first part of the dream described visions of wild beasts arising out of a tumultuous sea (Daniel 7:2–8). The second part of the dream showed God sitting on His heavenly throne as sovereign over these beasts (7:9–12). The third section of the dream portrayed the Son of Man's kingdom and dominion (7:13–14). And finally, Daniel asked for and received an interpretation of the vision (7:15–27).

Comparatively, Daniel 7 is quite similar to Daniel 2, which contains Nebuchadnezzar's dream of a giant statue. (The statue and Daniel's interpretation is discussed in detail in lesson 4 of *Daniel, Volume 1: God's Man for the Moment Bible Companion*.) The following chart compares these two chapters and their interpretations.

Daniel 2 *The Statue*	**Representative Kingdoms**	**Daniel 7** *The Beasts*
Golden head	Babylon	Winged lion
Silver chest and arms	Medo-Persia	Lopsided bear
Bronze belly and thighs	Greece	Four-headed leopard
Iron legs	Rome	Terrible beast
Iron/clay feet and toes	Western nations	Ten horns

Nebuchadnezzar dreamed of a stone that crushed the statue (Daniel 2:34–35, 44–45). Correspondingly, Daniel dreamed of the "Son of Man," the "Highest One," who will rule over the nations (7:13–14, 27).

THE VISION

Now that we have a pretty good grasp of the big picture, let's look at the details of Daniel's dream.

Read Daniel 7:2–8.

Lying on his bed asleep, Daniel received a dream filled with unusual visions (Daniel 7:1). He saw "the four winds of heaven"[5] whipping into a frenzy the "great sea," out of which came four unusual beasts (7:2–3).[6]

The first beast looked "like a lion [with] the wings of an eagle," symbolizing strength and swiftness (7:4). Archaeologists have discovered that the national symbol of Babylon was the winged lion, which is also attested to in Scripture (Jeremiah 50:17; Ezekiel 17:3, 12). Then the lion's wings were "plucked . . . and [it was] made to stand on two feet . . . [and it was given] a human mind" (Daniel 7:4). These metaphors signify the insanity of Nebuchadnezzar as well as his change of heart toward God.

The second beast resembled a lopsided bear with three ribs in its mouth (7:5). It had two legs that were shorter than the others. This indicated that the Persians, though rising later, would dominate the Medes in their united kingdom. Throughout Scripture, bears are known for their aggressive and carnivorous behavior (2 Samuel 17:8; 2 Kings 2:24; Hosea 13:8). The meaning of the three ribs in the bear's mouth is uncertain,[7] but it is clear that the Medo-Persians were ferocious as they gobbled up territory (Isaiah 13:15–18). They operated under the authority of God, who told them to "Arise, devour much meat!" (Daniel 7:5).

The third beast looked like a leopard with four wings and four heads (7:6). In the Bible, leopards are depicted as swift (Habakkuk 1:8) and cunning (Jeremiah 5:6; Hosea 13:7). This reflects the manner in which Alexander the Great and the Greeks conquered the Medo-Persian Empire and then the known world. After the death of Alexander in 323 BC, his kingdom was divided among four generals (see also Daniel 8:8, 21–22). As were Babylon and Medo-Persia, Greece was granted the authority to rule by the sovereignty of the Most High.

The fourth beast was unlike anything Daniel had ever seen before. It was "dreadful and terrifying and extremely strong" (7:7). Its teeth were large and like iron, and it "devoured and crushed and trampled down" the other beasts. This beast represented the Roman Empire, which destroyed Greece and conquered a wider range of territory than any of those who had come before.

On the fourth beast's head were ten horns, representing ten kings or kingdoms (7:7, 23–24). While Daniel was pondering the ten horns, an eleventh horn, a "little one," began to emerge from the midst of the others, uprooting three of the horns. The little horn was intelligent and had a mouth from which it blasphemed God (7:8). It represents the Antichrist, whom we'll study in more depth in a later chapter.

Why do you think God used such vivid, fantastic dreams and visions to communicate truth about the future to Daniel?

Do you think God's motive was to hide information or to reveal it?

 **Read Daniel 7:9–12.**

A predecessor to Daniel, the prophet Isaiah, called God "the high and exalted One / Who lives forever, whose name is Holy" (Isaiah 57:15). In the next part of his vision, Daniel called God "the Ancient of Days" (Daniel 7:9), referring to the truth that God is eternal. He then described how God will sit in sovereign judgment over the nations. Daniel was privileged to see God's holiness—His clothing was "like white snow / And the hair of His head like pure wool"—and to see God's awe-inspiring divine glory and judgment—"His throne was ablaze with flames, / Its wheels were a burning fire" (7:9).

The fiery wheels on God's throne in Daniel's vision were similar to another prophet's vision (Ezekiel 1:4–28). This image is hard to grasp with our finite minds, but the fiery wheels represent God's providential dealings with humanity and His holy justice. God is often spoken of as a "consuming fire" (Deuteronomy 4:24; Hebrews 12:29), and Daniel's vision indicated that rivers of fire flow like lava from His throne (Daniel 7:10).

One day God will open the books of judgment, which have recorded all the evil of humanity and the blasphemies from the little horn (see also Revelation 20:11–15), and He will rain down judgment and decimate the terrible beast (Daniel 7:10–11). The other beasts—the lion, bear, and leopard (which represent the other nations)—will have already been conquered, but their way of life will be allowed to continue for "an appointed period of time" (7:12).

In Daniel 7:12, who took away the beasts' dominion and determined the appointed time they would "be allowed" to live? What does this tell you about God's power over evil today?

____

____

____

Read Daniel 7:13–14.

While Daniel kept his gaze fixed upon the Ancient of Days, he saw "One like a Son of Man" riding on the clouds and approaching God (Daniel 7:13). "Son of Man" is a common name for the Messiah in Scripture. He was given power and authority to rule an eternal, worldwide kingdom. All "peoples, nations and men of every language" will serve Him forever (7:14).

When He was on earth, Jesus often called Himself "Son of Man." Based on Daniel 7:13–14, what details about Himself was He communicating to the people?

____

____

____

What other Bible verses or passages can you find that demonstrate the deity of Jesus?

____

____

____

Read Matthew 24:30; 26:64 (see also Mark 13:26; 14:62; Luke 21:27). Do Jesus's words confirm or deny the veracity of Daniel's writings? What do they tell you about Jesus's deity and sovereignty over the world?

___

___

___

THE INTERPRETATION

Read Daniel 7:15–27.

These visions left Daniel reeling (Daniel 7:15). Unable to make sense of what he had seen, he asked Gabriel, who was standing nearby, to help him understand.[8] The four beasts, Gabriel explained, were four kings who came out of the nations (7:16–17). Skipping over the fourth beast and fast-forwarding to the time when this beast had been judged, Gabriel also told Daniel that the "saints of the Highest One" would receive the kingdom (7:18).

Gabriel may have wanted to focus on the glorious divine kingdom, but Daniel was stuck on the details of the fourth beast and what the ten horns represented, especially the little horn with eyes and a blasphemous mouth (7:19–20). As Daniel watched, the little horn fought with the saints, "overpowering them" until God came and passed judgment. Then the "saints took possession of the kingdom" (7:21–22).

So Gabriel explained that the fourth beast was a powerful kingdom, devouring, tearing down, and crushing "the whole earth" (7:23). At the height of its power, Rome dominated much of the known world, but never the whole earth. The reference here is to a Roman-like world government in which a confederation of ten nations will rule until one king deposes three others and assumes authority over the remaining seven (Daniel 7:24).[9] This will take place in the end times after the church has been raptured and the tribulation begins.

The horn that arose from the midst of the ten and deposed three is a single individual—"he will speak out" (7:25). He is named the "Antichrist" (see 1 John 2:18, 22). By exalting himself, he will blaspheme God (2 Thessalonians 2:4). He will oppress God's people. He will attempt to change moral and natural laws. And he will rule from Israel's capital city, Jerusalem, for three and a half years (Daniel 11:45; Revelation 13:5).

After this time, the Ancient of Days will convene His court (Daniel 7:10), the Son of Man will come in battle array (see Revelation 19:11–12), and the Antichrist will be "annihilated and destroyed forever" (Daniel 7:26). Christ, the "Highest One," will then establish His millennial kingdom, ruling as Israel's King and the sovereign of all dominions (7:27).[10]

STARTING YOUR JOURNEY

Prophecies of strange beasts, a one-world dominion, and divine judgment can be frightening (Daniel 7:28). But if we take in the God-given truth in Daniel 7, we can rest peacefully, knowing that the Ancient of Days and the Son of Man are in complete control.

Historically, Daniel 7 teaches us that *because the first three kingdoms have been as God predicted, so will the fourth.*

Knowing that the first three beasts represent real, historical kingdoms, how should you interpret the other parts of Daniel's vision?

____

____

____

Next, we learn that *because the nations were established by God, they dwell under His sovereign control.*

How does God's sovereignty over "the nations" fit with the overarching theme of Daniel 1–6?

Personally, we can rest assured that *the God who has mapped out our future certainly is able to handle the present.*

Do you find it easier to trust God for your present circumstances or for your distant future? Explain.

The final personal lesson is that *though life may appear to be a collage, it is, in reality, the unfolding of God's perfect plan.*

We all would like to know the full picture of what God is doing in our lives, but He rarely lets us in on that information. Instead, He wants us to trust Him. Read Proverbs 3:5–6, and then write it in your own words.

Daniel was troubled and perplexed by the fantastic dreams and visions he received, and he struggled to understand God's message in this collage. Over time, we can see the bigger picture and discern that many of these predictions have been clearly fulfilled in history. God cares for us and wants us to know that His plan for the future will also be fulfilled. We can rest confidently in His sovereign control over the nations and over our individual lives.

LESSON TWO

THE FINAL WORLD DICTATOR

Selected Scriptures

THE HEART OF THE MATTER

Freedom brings both responsibility and risk. And because freedom carries such weight, people will often give up their freedom for security. Dictators prey on this tendency. And at no time in human history will this be more evident than during the terrible time of the great tribulation when the Antichrist rules the world.

The Bible speaks of this world dictator in great detail and challenges people to make a choice—either to accept freedom in Christ and trust in the security of everlasting life or to seek temporary security in the Antichrist and suffer everlasting spiritual enslavement.

DISCOVERING THE WAY

In his masterpiece, *The Brothers Karamazov*, Fyodor Dostoevsky places before his audience a legend called "The Grand Inquisitor," in which a penetrating question is asked—What will produce happiness: security or freedom? The story revolves around the Cardinal of Seville. He arrests a man who turns out to be Jesus. The Grand Inquisitor accuses Jesus of damning humanity to the misery of suffering. The Inquisitor reasons that by rejecting Satan's temptations, Christ made a way for humankind to freely choose obedience or rebellion. He then suggests that if Jesus had only succumbed to Satan, He could have brought paradise to earth. Humanity, the Inquisitor argues, can't handle the responsibilities of freedom. They crave security instead. The Inquisitor says,

> All that man seeks on earth . . . [is] someone to bow down to, someone to take over his conscience, and a means for uniting everyone at last into a common, concordant, and incontestable anthill.[1]

These three descriptions are an apt representation of what the Antichrist will accomplish during the tribulation. But before the end-time events begin, Christ's church, those who have accepted Christ as Lord, will be removed from the earth in what is commonly known as the rapture.[2]

First Thessalonians 4:15–17 describes the rapture. Read these verses and explain in your own words what will happen at that moment.

____

____

____

____

Who will be left on earth after the rapture? Why do you think the world will be thrown into chaos when Jesus removes believers from the earth?

____

____

____

____

Do you think the world will be ready for a worldwide dictator at that time? Why, or why not?

____

____

____

GENERAL INFORMATION ABOUT THE ANTICHRIST

Before we look at the particulars of who and what the Antichrist will be and will do, let's address some common misconceptions.

He will be wanted, not rejected. After the rapture, anarchy will reign on the earth. "In the twinkling of an eye" (1 Corinthians 15:52), millions upon millions of people will suddenly disappear. Thousands of others will be killed or injured when planes drop out of the sky and cars careen out of control. Banks will collapse; looting and violent crime will be epidemic. Governments around the world will be in disarray—impotent to halt the free fall of lawlessness and chaos. Everyone will long for someone to seize control and bring order out of disorder. And the Antichrist will fill that role.

He will be appealing, not repulsive. The Bible refers to the Antichrist as a blasphemous horn (Daniel 7:24–25), as lawless (2 Thessalonians 2:3–4), and as a beast (Revelation 13:1–2)—hardly attractive descriptions. But we know that people will follow him (13:3), so he will present himself as an alluring leader—at first.

GETTING TO THE ROOT
The Anti- in Antichrist

The word *Antichrist*, translated from *antichristos*, occurs only five times in the Bible, all of them used by John in his first two letters (1 John 2:18, 22; 4:3; 2 John 1:7). The prefix *anti-* is most commonly translated in English as it is in Greek—meaning "opposite" or opposed to something.[3] So *Antichrist* can be literally interpreted to mean "against Christ." This clearly fits his description—he will be a blasphemer (Daniel 7:25; Revelation 13:5–6).

However, the prefix *anti-* can also be rendered "instead of" or "in place of."[4] In this sense the Antichrist will seek to replace or mimic Christ, setting himself up as another messiah or savior, worthy of worship (Revelation 13:4). He will speak of peace, justice, unity, and order. His message and his manner, at least for a time, will be "Christlike." And that will be attractive indeed.

He will be super, not ordinary. Everything about the Antichrist will be extraordinary. He will possess the eloquence of Abraham Lincoln, the charm of John F. Kennedy, the wit of Winston Churchill, the military genius of Napoleon, the vision of Martin Luther King Jr., and the intelligence of Albert Einstein.

He will be a Gentile, not a Jew. The Bible indicates that the Antichrist will emerge out of "the sea" (Daniel 7:2–3; Revelation 13:1; see also lesson 1, note 6), indicating that he will arise out of the Gentile nations, not Israel.

The apostle John warned us that in the last days the "spirit of the antichrist" will increase and lead people away from the truth. Read 1 John 2:18–22; 4:2–3. What is the key to spotting an "antichrist," or false teacher—one who mimics the spirit of the worldwide dictator yet to come?

____

____

____

List some of today's popular religions, philosophies, or ideas that exhibit the "spirit of antichrist."

____

____

____

Why do you think these religions or philosophies attract followers?

____

____

____

SPECIFIC SCRIPTURES DESCRIBING THE ANTICHRIST

Don't you wish the Bible would name names when it comes to the Antichrist? Who exactly is he? It would be intriguing to know, but in the end it doesn't make much difference—it's *what* he is and does that is important. And the Bible gives more than enough information to answer that question.

Read Daniel 7:24–25.

Notice the Antichrist's almost imperceptible rise to power and his animosity toward God's saints.[5] He won't rise like a rocket, instantly taking his position as a worldwide dictator. Instead he will grow into power, like a horn growing on the head of an animal. Once in power, he will blaspheme God and persecute the saints (Daniel 7:25). Daniel 8:24–25 describes this clearly: "He will destroy mighty men and the holy people. . . . He will even oppose the Prince of princes"—Jesus Christ.

Let's turn away from Daniel for a moment to catch a glimpse of the Antichrist as he's mentioned throughout the New Testament.

Read 2 Thessalonians 2:1–4.

The Thessalonian believers were enduring persecution, and the false teachers used their circumstances to trumpet the judgment of the day of the Lord. The Thessalonian church feared that they had missed the rapture. Encouraging the Thessalonians, Paul told them not to worry because they were followers of Christ. "God has not destined [believers] for wrath" (1 Thessalonians 5:9). He told them not to be disturbed because the day of the Lord had yet to come. In fact, the final judgment will not come until a specific event occurs and a specific person is revealed. First must come "the apostasy"—open and worldwide rebellion against God (2 Thessalonians 2:3). The person who will lead this rebellion will be "the man of lawlessness . . . the son of destruction"—the Antichrist (2:3). He will be characterized as refusing "to conform to the law of God" or "to be ruled by God."[6] He will defy both moral laws and civil laws.

He will proudly oppose the Creator and exalt himself as if he were God. Entering the temple, he will present himself as worthy of worship (2 Thessalonians 2:4). The fulfillment of his self-deification is found in Revelation 13.

Read Revelation 13:1–4, 11–18.

Revelation 13:1–2 is very similar to Daniel 7:2–8. Look at each passage carefully, and list the similarities and differences.

Similarities	Differences

John's vision of a great beast arising from the Gentile nations mirrors Daniel's vision—ten horns representing the confederation of ten nations that will oppose God. John saw seven heads, probably corresponding to the original ten leaders Daniel saw, including the three that had been "pulled out by the roots" by the Antichrist (Daniel 7:8). The ten crowns represent governments and governmental authority (Revelation 13:1). John also included this curious detail: "The dragon gave [the beast] his power and his throne and great authority" (13:2). The dragon is Satan, the real power behind the puppet-authority of the Antichrist.[7]

Mysteriously, this beast, the Antichrist, who took on the characteristics of conquered nations,[8] will fall, possibly from an assassin's blow. The Beast will appear to die—John says that he saw the Antichrist "*as if* [he] had been slain" (Revelation 13:3, emphasis added). Satan will counterfeit Christ's resurrection by healing the Beast's wound, duping the world into thinking that he had risen from the dead.[9] After his "miraculous" resuscitation, the entire world—in astonishment—will worship "the dragon . . . [and] the beast" (13:4).

John saw another beast (13:11) who is later identified as the False Prophet (19:20). In the midst of worldwide chaos, the False Prophet will use his authority and power to perform unusual signs, deceiving the people into a false hope and into worshiping an image of the Antichrist (13:12–14). Those who refuse to worship will be killed (13:15).

After the rapture, the world's economy will crash. The False Prophet, along with the Antichrist, will stabilize it by strict control over who can buy and sell. Every man, woman, and child will receive a mark, without which one cannot participate, leading to great suffering for those who refuse it. The mark will either be "the name of the beast or the number of his name . . . six hundred and sixty-six" (13:17–18).[10]

Whomever the Antichrist turns out to be, his doom is sure, as Revelation 19 promises.

Read Revelation 19:19–21.

At the culmination of time, the armies of the Antichrist will form in battle array against Christ (19:11–19). Christ will lay hold of the Beast and the False Prophet and consign them to the lake of fire (19:20). The remaining rebels who took the mark of the beast will be killed by a word from Christ's mouth (19:21), ending the evil reign of the "little horn" that Daniel saw, the Antichrist.

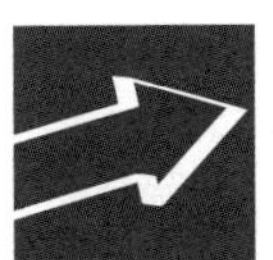

STARTING YOUR JOURNEY

What can believers, who'll be raptured before the advent of the Antichrist, glean from learning about the life and activities of this evil man? Take these three lessons to heart—two involve discerning the times and one anticipates the rescue of Christ's church.

When you watch the news, keep a keen eye on the Middle East. Though the followers of Christ will be raptured before the Antichrist is revealed, the epicenter of end times events will be Israel. And as you see and hear of "wars and rumors of wars" (Matthew 24:6), *keep your perspective by interpreting current events in light of prophetic truth.*

What events are currently happening in the Middle East? When you think about them, what words or phrases come to mind?

____

____

____

Second Timothy 3:1–4 provides a vivid description of the attitudes that will be exhibited in the last days. In what ways are these characteristics evident today?

____

____

____

Paying attention to the Middle East and filtering those events through the Scriptures is important in order to keep a healthy perspective on the last days and the activities of the Antichrist. But the importance of these pale in comparison with *our commitment to anticipate Christ's coming and trust in God's promise of the rapture.*

Read 2 Timothy 4:8. Would you characterize yourself as a person who loves the Lord's "appearing"? Please explain.

____

____

____

Although Romans 10:9–10 doesn't speak of the rapture, it does prescribe what you must do to be prepared for the rapture. What do these verses say?

____

____

____

____

Are you prepared for the rapture?

Yes	No

If you are unsure, please read "How to Begin a Relationship with God" at the end of this Bible Companion.

It appears that Dostoevsky's Grand Inquisitor was correct. For the sake of security, humanity will one day follow the False Prophet and bow to worship Satan and the Antichrist; they'll freely give up their consciences and blithely follow the evil trinity[11] into the lake of fire. But we don't have to become part of the Antichrist's "anthill." We can find freedom and security by trusting in Christ, ensuring that we are ready for the rapture.

LESSON THREE

THE LIVING END

Daniel 8

THE HEART OF THE MATTER

Two years elapsed between Daniel's vision in chapter 7 and his vision in chapter 8. Like the former, this vision involves animals. But unlike it, this one provides great detail about some of the most famous leaders in history and about the one who will be the most nefarious man in history, whose time is yet to come. To Daniel, this was all future. To us, much of it is history—a history worth studying, not just for the sake of knowledge, but to give us confidence in God's sovereignty. This history will also encourage us to warn non-Christians of the future that awaits them.

DISCOVERING THE WAY

The chart of history is meant to be studied. The foolish forget and suffer the panic of becoming unmoored. The wise remember and find a sure compass. Or as Chuck Colson wisely put it,

> Disdaining the past and its values, we flee the judgment of the dead. We tear down memory's monuments—removing every guidepost and landmark—and wander in unfamiliar country. But it is a sterile wasteland in which men and women are left with carefully furnished lives and utterly barren souls.[1]

For many, history is a subject they'd just as soon forget. But forgetfulness can lead to paralyzing fear, especially when facing an uncertain future. Remembering, on the other hand, can bring confidence and assurance.

What is one practical lesson you've learned from history? Explain.

____

____

____

____

Do you consider history (global or personal) when you make decisions? If yes, give an example. If no, why not?

____

____

____

____

THE VISION

Something interesting happens when we turn the page in our Bibles to Daniel 8. If we were reading this in the original language, we'd immediately notice that Aramaic, the language of the Gentiles, gives way to Hebrew. This shift signifies that from this point forward, Daniel's prophecies will focus on the nation of Israel.

 **Read Daniel 8:1–2.**

"In the third year of the reign of Belshazzar" (Daniel 8:1), two years after his first vision, Daniel had another.[2] Rather than Daniel's adopted home of Babylon, the setting of this one was the "citadel of Susa . . . in the province of Elam . . . beside the Ulai Canal" (8:2).[3]

It's easy to overlook these seemingly small details, but the fact that Daniel saw himself in Susa—the future capital of Persia—is significant. The vision concerns, at least initially, the Persian Empire, which would not come to the height of its power for another decade or so.

Read Daniel 8:3–14.

Daniel saw a ram standing by the canal. It had two horns on its head—one longer than the other. Coming out of the east, the ram conquered lands in the west, north, and south. No one could stop the swift attack of his butting head, and he became powerful.

As he was paying close attention to the ram, Daniel's concentration was suddenly arrested by a "male goat" coming out of the west. It traveled so fast that its feet never touched the ground. The goat also had a horn, but this one was quite large and sat right in the middle of its forehead (8:5). Charging with rage, the goat "struck the ram and shattered his two horns." Knocking it to the ground, the goat "trampled" the ram (8:6–7).

The goat gloated in his victory over the ram. But at the height of his power, the goat's large horn was mysteriously broken. In its place, "four conspicuous horns [grew] toward the four winds of heaven" (8:8).

Next, Daniel watched as another horn grew out from the goat's head. This "rather small horn[4] . . . grew exceedingly great toward the south, . . . the east, and . . . the Beautiful Land"—Israel (8:9). With its attention focused on Israel, the vision predicted that the small horn would persecute God's chosen people, the Jews (8:10), declare itself equal to the Most High, "the Commander of the host" (8:11), halt temple sacrifices and desecrate God's holy house (8:11), subjugate the Jews into worshiping it (8:12), and despise the truth—the

Word of God (Daniel 8:12). The small horn would do as it pleases and initially have great success.

Reread Daniel 8:9–12. What would you say is the key theme underlying the events?

____

____

____

What does Numbers 28:2–8 tell us about sacrifices made to the Lord?

____

____

____

What did the small horn attempt to do to the relationship between God and His people?

____

____

____

Suddenly, Daniel heard the voices of two "holy ones" speaking and was immediately riveted by their conversation. "How long," one angel said to another, "will . . . the transgression [cause] horror, so as to allow both the holy place and the host to be trampled?" (8:13). The answer came back, "2,300 evenings and mornings." At the end of that time, "the holy place will be properly restored" (8:14).

What could this mean? The chronology of creation uses the same formula to indicate days (Genesis 1:5). Perhaps, however, it's best to view the angel's statement not as days but as different times when sacrifices were offered—twice a day. This interpretation is especially compelling given the context of Daniel 8:9–12.

THE INTERPRETATION

As soon as the vision faded, Daniel tried to understand what it meant. Fortunately, for him, and for us as well, God sent the angel Gabriel to give the interpretation.

Read Daniel 8:15–19.

A voice commanded the angel Gabriel to "give this man an understanding of the vision" (Daniel 8:16).[5] When Gabriel approached, Daniel fell down in awe. Gabriel said to him, "Son of man, understand that the vision pertains to the time of the end" (8:17).[6] As Gabriel was speaking, Daniel fell asleep—still prostrate before the angel—until Gabriel helped him to his feet. The angel then repeated his mission; he was there to help Daniel understand what will take place at "the appointed time of the end" (8:19).

Gabriel used the phrase "time of the end" twice when speaking with Daniel about this vision. Why do you think this is significant?

____

____

____

Before we rush on to the details of the interpretation, let's reorient ourselves. What Gabriel told Daniel was completely prophetic and future to Daniel. As we read these verses today, some of the prophecy has now turned to history, and other particulars of the prophecy remain to be fulfilled in the future. Students of Scripture understand this as a "double fulfillment"—God revealed specifics about a now historical individual, who was yet unborn during Daniel's lifetime. And in the process of this revelation, the Lord gave a foreshadowing of an individual yet to come who has many of the same characteristics as the historical person.

THE VISION FULFILLED IN HISTORY

Read Daniel 8:20–26.

Gabriel started explaining at the beginning, with the ram and the male goat. The ram was Medo-Persia (Daniel 8:20). Remember the lopsided bear in Daniel 7:5? The two horns in Daniel 8:20 represent the same consolidated kingdom. The first horn (Media) was dwarfed by the slower growing but more significant horn (Persia). The goat represented Greece, and the horn that grew out of the goat's head represented Greece's "first king" (Daniel 8:21)—Alexander the Great.[7]

Marching out of the west in 334 BC, Alexander would not be deterred from his ambition to conquer the world. With lightning speed (8:5), Alexander trampled over the Medo-Persian Empire (8:6–7) in three short years, when he defeated Darius III at Gaugamela. After the defeat of Persia, Alexander continued his conquest of Asia, pushing eastward into India. His weary soldiers, though, had had enough of warfare and pressed him to cease his conquest. Returning to Babylon, Alexander died in 323 BC, at the height of his power—"as soon as he was mighty" (8:8). He was 32 years old.

When Alexander died, his kingdom was divided among four of his generals—the "four horns" of Daniel 8:22. Ptolemy ruled Egypt, Seleucus controlled Babylon, Lysimachus governed much of Asia Minor, and Cassander ruled Greece.[8] After many years of warfare among themselves and their descendants, a king arose—the small horn of verse 9—"in the latter period of their rule" (8:23). History identifies this small horn, this "insolent" man, as the Seleucid king Antiochus IV Epiphanes, who came to power in 175 BC.[9]

Egypt, under the rule of Ptolemy VI, declared war on Antiochus around 170 BC. Moving swiftly, Antiochus counterattacked, defeated the Egyptian army, and marched on to Memphis. Ptolemy then negotiated a peace treaty. On Antiochus's return to Antioch, he looted the temple at Jerusalem.

Two years later, in 168 BC, Antiochus saw what he thought were favorable conditions to solidify his control over Ptolemy. The Romans, who were growing in power, had a treaty with Egypt that bound them to protect Ptolemy from aggression. But the Romans were fighting in Macedonia, and Antiochus assumed that they would be occupied there. So he set off for Egypt—his growth "toward the south" (Daniel 8:9).[10]

His plans were foiled by the intervention of Rome, and Antiochus retreated in anger. Moving through Israel, he killed many and took others captive (8:9–10). Preventing the Jews from observing the law of Moses regarding Sabbaths, festival days, and diet (8:11), he also punished mothers who had their sons circumcised and destroyed the sacred scrolls—"fling[ing] truth to the ground" (8:12). In the ultimate act of rebellion, Antiochus built an idol, possibly to Zeus, on God's altar in the temple and sacrificed a pig on it.[11] Other pagan altars were set up throughout the city, and on December 17, 167 BC, the Jews were ordered to sacrifice and eat swine or face death.[12]

But just as the angel had predicted in Daniel 8:13–14, three years after Antiochus desecrated the temple, it was restored and the holy sacrifice was resumed on a new altar (8:14).[13]

THE FULFILLMENT YET TO COME

Antiochus cast a shadow for the Antichrist, giving us a glimpse of who is to come. The Antichrist will arise at the end of time, when the sins of humanity "have run their course" (8:23). He will be intelligent and cunning (8:23) and have great Satanic power (8:24). He will persecute all who refuse to worship him, especially God's "holy people," the Jews (8:24). He will deceive many into following him, but he will later destroy them (8:25). The Antichrist will also declare himself to be a god, in opposition to Christ, "the Prince of princes" (8:25). And he will be "broken," but not by human hands.[14] Christ will one day consign the Antichrist to the lake of fire (Revelation 19:20).

Gabriel assured Daniel that the interpretation was true and that he should keep it in mind, "for it pertains to many days in the future" (Daniel 8:26).

STARTING YOUR JOURNEY

Daniel's response to the vision and interpretation was utter exhaustion and sickness, preventing him from carrying out his official duties for a time. And though Gabriel explained the meaning of the vision, it still didn't make sense to Daniel (Daniel 8:27).

Our response to the vision and interpretation, no doubt, is different from Daniel's. Part of it has already been fulfilled, and we also have the rest of the Bible to provide context. But regardless of what we think about this astonishing chapter, we can learn at least two lessons from it.

First, the fulfillment of Daniel's vision in the historical person of Antiochus should *help you gain confidence in God's Word*. If prophecy can become history, as it did with Antiochus, then we can trust that what God says about the future will one day also become history.

If you were to explain to others why they could or should have confidence in the Scriptures, what might you say?

____

____

____

____

Sometimes confidence in the truth of the Scriptures, especially when it speaks of the activities of the Antichrist, can lead to fear—either for ourselves or for those we love. So we need to learn that *there is great hope in Christ*, for we have eternal security in Him.

Jesus speaks of the coming tribulation in Revelation 3:10 and offers a magnificent word of hope for those who follow Him. What is it?

Who will escape the testing hour and who will have to endure it, according to Revelation 3:10?

Do you know someone who, if the rapture occurred today, wouldn't escape the "hour of testing"? If so, who? And what would you tell that person so he or she might have the hope of escape?

We study history not for mere knowledge but because it has value for our lives—warning us of error and pointing us to right. The great Greek historian Thucydides wisely understood that what happened in the past by virtue of human nature will happen in the future. He wrote,

> If [his chronicle of history] be judged useful by those inquirers who desire an exact knowledge of the past as an aid to the understanding of the future . . . I shall be content. . . . I have written my work, not as an essay which is to win the applause of the moment, but as a possession for all time.[15]

Daniel's vision was not preserved to win the applause of the moment, but as a possession for all time. It serves as a warning to those without the hope of Christ of the future awaiting them and challenges those of us who have that hope to share it.

LESSON FOUR

TRUE CONFESSIONS

Daniel 9:1–19

THE HEART OF THE MATTER

When nations move away from the faith that helped establish them, decay is not far behind. For Americans, "In God We Trust" and "One Nation under God" have become hollow, proverbial sayings that describe the American character . . . of yesteryear. In recent decades, these ideas have come under mounting attack as a violation of the constitutional separation of church and state. Almost imperceptibly, our religious heritage has eroded and left us with an increasingly secular society.

Daniel clearly understood that a nation or empire that forgets God is destined to eventually become a disgrace—a footnote in the pages of history. So at the dawn of a new administration in the land, Daniel prayed for his people, Israel. And from his knees, Daniel once again gave us an example to follow—that of a true patriot who earnestly prays for his country.

DISCOVERING THE WAY

Samuel Davies is not a familiar name to most of us. He was one of the most influential preachers in pre Revolutionary War Virginia, inspiring the likes of Patrick Henry. Davies fervently believed in mixing Christianity and patriotism when the times called for it. On July 20, 1755, the time had come. He exhorted an audience to pray for Virginia after the defeat and death of British General Braddock at the hands of the French and Indians at Fort Duquesne. He thundered,

> We ought not indeed to content ourselves with lazy prayers; it is our duty also to take all the measures in our power to prevent or escape the impending ruin of our country; but it is certainly our duty to humble ourselves before that God whom we have offended, and to cry mightily to him [so that perhaps] he may yet have mercy upon us that we perish not.[1]

How many of us are guilty of "lazy prayers" regarding the state of our country? How many have failed to humble ourselves and cry out mightily for God's mercy on our people and our leaders?

How often do you pray for your country and/or its leaders?

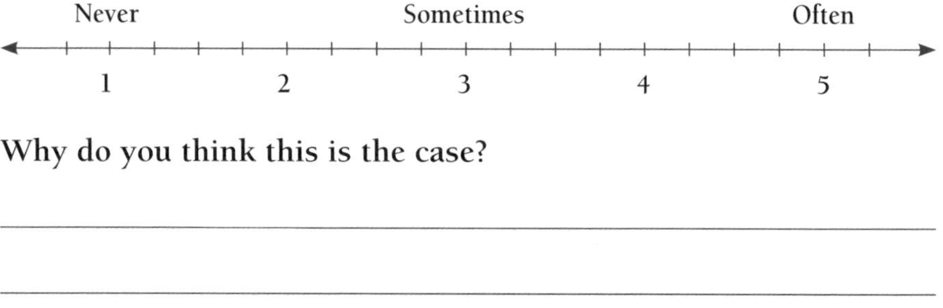

Why do you think this is the case?

THE SETTING FOR DANIEL'S PRAYER

No one could accuse Daniel of offering lazy prayers. Daniel 6:10 tells us that he knelt before God three times a day. Daniel 9:1–19 gives us the content of one of those prayers.

 **Read Daniel 9:1–2.**

When Babylon fell to the Medes and Persians in 539 BC, the situation was ripe for drastic change in regard to Daniel and the Jews. By that time, Daniel had been advising Babylonian kings for sixty-seven years, and he was in his late seventies or early eighties. What use would Darius, the new ruler, have for him?[2] More important, how would this new administration treat the people he loved so dearly?

So in the very "first year" of this new government (Daniel 9:1), Daniel sat down with a scroll containing the prophecies of Jeremiah and knelt before the Lord in prayer. While reading the sacred text, Daniel came across a specific prophecy pertaining to the length of the Jews' exile in Babylon (Jeremiah 25:8–12). He understood that these verses spoke directly to the Jews' current situation . . . and their immediate future.

Read Jeremiah 25:8–12. What specifically did the prophet say would happen to God's people? Whom would they serve? For how long? And what would happen to that nation?

____

____

____

____

Every word in the book of Jeremiah had come true up to that point, and Daniel was confident that God would bring His people back to their homeland after seventy years were completed (Daniel 9:2).[3]

THE INGREDIENTS IN DANIEL'S PRAYER

Daniel could do the math. The "desolation of Jerusalem," when the Babylonian army destroyed Jerusalem and took Daniel and others captive, had occurred in 605 BC. Daniel was reading the prophecies of Jeremiah in 538 BC. Nearly seventy years had passed. The time of fulfillment was at hand. So Daniel prayed for his people.

 **Read Daniel 9:3–6.**

Daniel said, "I gave my attention to the Lord God to seek Him" (Daniel 9:3). With intense *concentration*, Daniel worshipfully came before God, confessing his nation's sins. In *supplication*, Daniel laid his heart and mind bare before the Lord, asking for mercy. With *fasting*—refusing to eat for a time so to give priority to prayer—Daniel sought God on behalf of Israel. In *humility*, grieving over the sins of his nation, Daniel wore traditional mourning clothes of rough sackcloth and threw ashes on his head. And with complete *honesty*, Daniel contrasted God's faithfulness with the faithlessness of the nation—including his own.

GETTING TO THE ROOT

A Litany of Sins

Daniel knew that his nation had much to answer for, and he confessed the grossness of its sins in five different ways (Daniel 9:5). First, Daniel said Israel "sinned"; here he used the Hebrew word *chata*. This term reflects the general idea of "do[ing] wrong, commit[ting] a mistake." It is often translated as "miss[ing] the mark."[4] They had failed to meet God's standard of holiness.

They also "committed iniquity." This Hebrew word used here, *avah*, means to "bend" or "twist." It can also be translated as "perverted of mind."[5] The people's hearts and minds had turned away from the things of God.

Daniel then confessed that they had acted "wickedly," or *rasha*. This word usually refers to criminal acts or the violation of civil, ethical, and religious laws.[6]

Israel had also "rebelled" against God. They had *marad*, "attack[ed]" or "run strenuously" away from God.[7]

Finally, Israel had "turn[ed] aside" from following God's commandments. The Hebrew word used here is *sur*—they had become apostates.[8]

As if the litany of sins in Daniel 9:5 weren't enough, Daniel confessed that he and the nation had ignored God's prophets. They had not listened to the ones who warned Israel's "kings . . . princes . . . fathers and all the people" about God's impending judgment (Daniel 9:6).

Take a few moments and think about your native land. What sins have you and your country's people committed?

____

____

____

____

Go to the Lord on behalf of your city, state, and country, confessing these sins and asking for forgiveness.

PRAISE AFTER DANIEL'S CONFESSION

Turning his attention away from Israel's sins, Daniel then praised the Lord, focusing on both God's character and His deeds.

 **Read Daniel 9:7–15.**

First, *God is righteous*. The Lord was justified in disciplining Israel by casting them out of the Promised Land and scattering them to faraway places. They had been unfaithful and deserved their punishment (Daniel 9:7–8).

Second, *God is compassionate and forgiving*. Even though the people of Israel had rebelled, had been disobedient and stubborn, had refused to listen to the prophets, and had violated God's Law (9:9–11), God chose to forgive. He didn't pour out His complete wrath upon them, promising instead to restore them to the land after seventy years.

Third, *God is faithful*. He was faithful in carrying out what He had promised. Jerusalem was sacked, and the people were scattered. And yet, Daniel declared, the nation had remained obstinate and wouldn't confess their sins and seek God's mercy (Daniel 9:12–13). God was "righteous with respect to all His deeds which He has done," because Israel would not obey "His voice" (9:14).

In what ways have you seen God show these three characteristics to your nation?

Righteousness

____

____

____

Compassion and Forgiveness

____

____

____

Faithfulness

____

____

____

Pause here and thank God for His activity in and mercy toward your country.

THE MOTIVE BEHIND DANIEL'S PRAYER

Again Daniel confessed the nation's sins, but then he rehearsed God's faithfulness in bringing Israel out of Egypt and making His name great in the eyes of His people and the surrounding nations (Daniel 9:15). Daniel trusted that if God had acted in such magnificent ways to glorify Himself in the past, then God would certainly act in the future by fulfilling His promise to restore the nation and bringing glory to His name once again.

Read Daniel 9:16–19.

Daniel began this next part of his prayer with a "state of the union" analysis. The city of Jerusalem, the temple, and the whole nation had "become a reproach"—a laughingstock—to all the nations around them (9:16). Daniel called on God to turn His anger and wrath away and act in accordance with His promise. Only then would the nation reflect the glory of God to all those around it.

Second Chronicles 7:14 is addressed to God's people and outlines four requirements for national blessing. What are they?

1. ______________________________

2. ______________________________

3. ______________________________

4. ______________________________

What did God promise?

____

____

____

Daniel then petitioned the Lord, "So now . . . listen to the prayer of Your servant and to his supplications" (Daniel 9:17). For the sake of God's reputation, Daniel pleaded, "Let Your face shine on Your desolate sanctuary," the temple. Daniel asked God to look with compassion on the desolation of the nation and of God's own city, Jerusalem. Israel had no merit upon which to gain God's favor, but Daniel came to the Lord based on God's compassion alone (9:18).

Daniel ended his prayer with a call to action. "O Lord, hear! O Lord, forgive! O Lord, listen and take action! . . . do not delay" (9:19).

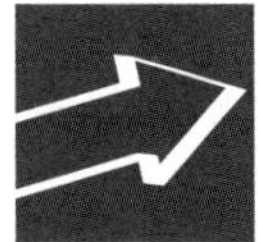

STARTING YOUR JOURNEY

In the frigid winter of 1776, George Washington's army shivered on the verge of annihilation. Writer Thomas Paine, in an effort to boost the troops' morale wrote,

> These are the times that try men's souls: The summer soldier and the sunshine patriot will, in this crisis, shrink from the service of his country; but he that stands it NOW, deserves the love and thanks of man and woman.[9]

Daniel lived during a time that tried the souls of his countrymen and women, but he didn't shrink from rendering the service of prayer for his nation. The times in which we live are also trying—crime, poverty, pornography, divorce, and war. We often feel helpless, like we can't possibly make a difference or bring about change. But that's not true. We can pray, bringing our sins and needs before the sovereign God who rules over all nations and peoples (Psalm 22:28). Prayer is the most powerful and effective way to serve our country (see James 5:16). Who will answer this call? Will you? Will you pray every day for your city, state, and nation?

Bad news bombards us every day, numbing our senses. But in order to begin praying for our communities, we must pay attention to the events taking place around us. Read your local newspaper or watch your local newscast, and write down some of the issues currently challenging your community.

____

____

____

____

Spend just a minute or two in prayer for a few of these news items.

Consider the leaders of your city, state, and country. Read the following verses and summarize what each one says about authority.

Proverbs 21:1 ______________________________

Romans 13:1 ______________________________

1 Timothy 2:1–2 ______________________________

1 Peter 2:13–14 ______________________________

Understanding what the Bible says about those in authority and our response to them, how can you pray for the leaders of your city, state, and country? List at least five names along with your ideas.

____

____

____

____

____

Offer a prayer right now, asking God to bring wisdom and justice to those whom He has placed in positions of authority.

During the contentious days when America was attempting to form a new constitution, a surprising proposal arose—surprising because it came from Benjamin Franklin, one of the least religious men in the room that day. Addressing George Washington, president of the Constitutional Convention, he said,

> "How has it happened, Sir, that we have not hitherto once thought of humbly applying to the Father of lights to illuminate our understandings? . . . I have lived, Sir, a long time, and the longer I live the more convincing proofs I see of this truth: that God governs in the affairs of men. And if a sparrow cannot fall to the ground without His notice, is it probable that an empire can rise without His aid?" [10]

Can an empire or nation flourish without God's aid? Look at your own country to answer that question. Let's commit ourselves, as Daniel did, to humbly petition the Lord for His forgiveness and blessings on our land. To make a real difference, we need to get on our knees!

LESSON FIVE

THE BACKBONE OF BIBLICAL PROPHECY

Daniel 9:20–27

THE HEART OF THE MATTER

The visions and dreams of Daniel's prophecies are incredibly complex. But perhaps none is more integral to understanding God's plan for His people than the one found in the last few verses of Daniel 9 . . . and certainly none is more difficult to follow. Daniel had Gabriel to help him navigate through the twists and turns of each prophetic word. We'll rely on the Holy Spirit and the rest of God's Word for insight and understanding as we learn more about the fulfillment of prophecy and as we're encouraged to trust in God's promises.

DISCOVERING THE WAY

Lewis Carroll, in his whimsical and strange children's tale *Through the Looking Glass*, relays a delightful exchange between Alice and the White Queen regarding "sums." " 'Can you do Addition?' the White Queen asked. 'What's one and one and one and one and one and one and one and one and one and one?' 'I don't know,' said Alice. 'I lost count.' "[1]

Math is one of those subjects that elicits either love or hatred—but rarely a shrug of the shoulders. Whether you love or hate math, our challenge, as we work our way through the extended word problem in the last four verses of Daniel 9, is to avoid losing count. And at the end of the problem, the practical application will add up.

Let's practice a math problem. (7 x 7) + (62 x 7) = x, and x + (3.5 x 2) = y. What are x and y? You can work out the problem in the box below.[2] (Go ahead and try; you'll find out why this is important later in the lesson.)

BACKGROUND AND INTRODUCTION

When last we left Daniel, he was kneeling in concentrated prayer for the nation of Israel.

Skim Daniel 9:1–19.

Daniel's prayer included a confession of sin, a review of God's character, and a petition. Outline Daniel's prayer, giving some details about each of these elements.

Read Daniel 9:20–23.

Daniel was weary, perhaps from the day's toil and certainly from the troubling thought that, though the seventy years of Jeremiah's prophecy (Jeremiah 25:11; Daniel 9:2) were almost complete, Israel was still in rebellion against God. And as he knelt and prayed fervently to God, the angel Gabriel suddenly interrupted and stood before Daniel in the form of a man (Daniel 9:20–21). Gabriel had come to give Daniel *sakal*, or "insight," and *binah*, or "understanding" (9:22).[3]

The first words of Daniel's prayer had barely escaped his mouth when Gabriel was dispatched from heaven to Daniel's side. He announced that Daniel was "highly esteemed," so the Lord would help him "gain understanding of the vision" to come (9:23).

Daniel had Gabriel to help him understand what was to come. According to John 14:26, who do Christians have to help them understand God's Word?

____

____

____

Pause here and ask the Lord to give you insight and understanding into His Word regarding the complicated prophecy of Daniel 9:24–27.

GENERAL FACTS

Bible scholar Donald Campbell observed that Daniel 9 is "Often called 'the backbone of prophecy' . . . rich with meaning."[4] Understanding these critical verses of what Gabriel told Daniel will straighten and strengthen our view of what God has done and will do for Israel.

Read Daniel 9:24–27.

Let's begin with some general observations. Notice, first, *a specific period of time is marked out by God*—"seventy weeks" (Daniel 9:24). Literally, this phrase is translated as seventy "periods of seven."[5] Because Daniel had been thinking in terms of years when he read Jeremiah's prophecy regarding the nation's seventy years of exile (9:2), it is best to view each of these periods of time as seven years.[6] Thus, the seventy "sevens" would equal 490 years.

Next, observe that *the prophecy is directly related to the Jews and Jerusalem*, not the church or the world. Gabriel said, "Seventy weeks have been decreed for *your people* and *your holy city*" (9:24, emphasis added).

Finally, *the total scene being revealed will last exactly seventy weeks*, again, 490 years. Gabriel told Daniel that the seventy weeks would be divided into sections of "seven weeks," "sixty-two weeks," and "one week" (9:25–27).

To keep our numbers straight, what did we say a "week" represented?

____

Multiply that number by each of the periods of time Gabriel told Daniel. Added together, what is the sum?[7]

Seven weeks equals ______________________________

Sixty-two weeks equals ___________________________

One week equals ________________________________

Total weeks equals ______________________________

Keep these calculations in mind as we dig into the details of Gabriel's explanation. But before we look at the particulars, review the following chart carefully.

The Seventy Weeks of Daniel 9:24–27

Artaxerxes's Decree (Nehemiah 2:1–8)	*Jerusalem Rebuilt* (Daniel 9:25)	*Triumphal Entry* (Luke 19:28–42)	*Jerusalem Destroyed* (Luke 19:43–44)	*Antichrist's Covenant with Israel* (Daniel 9:27)	*Antichrist's Covenant Broken* (Matthew 24:15)	*Christ's Second Coming* (Revelation 19:11–16)

"The Issuing of a Decree" (9:25)	"Restore and Rebuild Jerusalem" (9:25)	✝ Christ "Cut Off" (9:26)	War to the End (9:26)	"A Firm Covenant" (9:27)	"A Stop to Sacrifice and Grain Offering" (9:27)
7 weeks	62 weeks	Church Age		1 week	
(49 years)	(434 years)			(3.5 years)	(3.5 years)

444 BC — AD 33 — AD 70 — ?

SPECIFIC DETAILS

As we've already seen, the seventy weeks equals 490 years. But what will take place during these years? According to Daniel 9:24, six objectives will be accomplished. The first three deal with Israel's sin, and the second three address Israel's future.[8]

Israel's Sin

In Old Testament times, Israel's high priest offered sacrifices to atone for the sins of the nation, reconciling the people to God (see Leviticus 16). But each sacrifice was only a temporary provision—it had to be repeated again and again because Israel kept sinning. God sent His Son, Jesus Christ, to be sacrificed on the cross, providing the ultimate atonement for sin for those who believe in faith. But sin will continue to be evident in the world until Jesus comes again. At that time, God will:

1. "Finish the transgression"—bring an end to Israel's rebellion against God's Messiah
2. "Make an end of sin"—persuade Israel to turn away from its sin
3. "Make atonement for iniquity"—forgive Israel's sin through the work of the Messiah, Jesus, and restore the people of Israel into right relationship with Him

Israel's Kingdom

The second group of three accomplishments is also yet future. When Christ returns and establishes His millennial kingdom, God will:

1. "Bring in everlasting righteousness"—establish an age of righteousness
2. "Seal up vision and prophecy"—completely fulfill all prophetic Scriptures

3. "Anoint the most holy"—which could refer to the dedication of the millennial temple (Ezekiel 41–46) or to the enthronement of Christ as King (see Revelation 19:11–16)

These six accomplishments will fulfill God's covenants to Israel (Genesis 15:18–21; 2 Samuel 7:16; Jeremiah 31:31–34), bringing all of His promised blessings to the nation.

TELLING TIME

Gabriel told Daniel that the period of time "from the issuing of a decree to restore and rebuild Jerusalem" until the appearance of Christ would constitute forty-nine years ("seven weeks") and 434 years ("sixty-two weeks") (Daniel 9:25).[9] On March 5, 444 BC, in the time of Nehemiah, Artaxerxes Longimanus of Persia issued a decree to rebuild Jerusalem (Nehemiah 2:1–8).[10] Nehemiah recorded in his journal that the walls of Jerusalem were rebuilt in fifty-two days, and then families were required to live in the city (6:15; 11:1). Then, for the next forty-nine years (444 BC–395 BC), debris from Nebuchadnezzar's destruction was cleared, houses were built, and "streets and a trench" (Daniel 9:25 NIV) were constructed. This period of time corresponds to the first "seven weeks."

After these forty-nine years, a new era began—the "sixty-two weeks" or 434 years. Gabriel informed Daniel that at the end of this next period, "Messiah the Prince" (9:25) would appear. Fulfilling this prophecy exactly, Christ presented Himself to the nation of Israel as Messiah on March 30, AD 33, when He rode into Jerusalem on the foal of a donkey.[11] This event ended the "sixty-two weeks."

DOORWAY TO HISTORY

Differences in the Jewish and Modern Calendars

The prophecy's precision in dating both Artaxerxes's decree (444 BC) and Christ's triumphal entry (AD 33) is impressive. However, a difficulty arises when applying the 483 years in Daniel 9:25 (49 years plus 434 years) to these dates: it appears that Christ entered Jerusalem in AD 39 rather than AD 33. The math simply doesn't add up. We can reconcile this difference, however, by comparing the Jewish and Gregorian (modern) calendars.[12]

Jewish Calendar		**Modern Calendar**	
(360-day year)		*(365-day year)*	
(7 x 7) + (62 x 7) years = 483 years		444 BC to AD 33 = 476 years[13]	
483	years	476	Years
x 360	days	x 365	Days
173,880	days	173,740	Days
		+ 116	days in leap years[14]
		+ 24	days (March 5–March 30)[15]
		173,880	Days

According to Gabriel, at the *end* of the sixty-two weeks, "the Messiah will be cut off and have nothing" (Daniel 9:26). Forsaken by friends and even His Father (Matthew 27:46), Christ was crucified, died, and was buried. Then He rose again, overcoming death. His work provides atonement and salvation for all who would trust in Him (see John 3:16; 1 John 1:9).

The seven weeks and the sixty-two weeks (sixty-nine weeks total) ran consecutively. But there is a gap, an indefinite period of time, between the sixty-ninth and the seventieth weeks. This gap, though unknown to Daniel, is the current church age, as prophesied by Jesus (Matthew 16:18). At the time of His ascension into heaven, Jesus instituted the church age, which will last until the rapture.

Also, Gabriel said that during this gap prior to the seventieth week, "the people of the prince who is to come will destroy" Jerusalem and the temple (Daniel 9:26). This event occurred in AD 70 when the Roman general Titus ordered his legionnaires to lay waste to Jerusalem.[16] The history of Israel confirms that this period has been one of "war" and "desolations" as promised (9:26).

The sixty-nine weeks are history to us, but the seventieth week is yet to be. The clock will start on this last seven-year period, also called the tribulation, as soon as Christ raptures His church (1 Thessalonians 4:13–17). During that time, the Antichrist will emerge on the world's stage, and "he will make a firm covenant" with Israel "for one week"—seven years (Daniel 9:27). Apparently, the peace treaty the Antichrist will make with Israel will allow them to rebuild the temple and begin offering sacrifices according to Old Testament customs.[17] However, in the middle of this seven-year period, the Antichrist will violate this treaty and "will put a stop to sacrifice and grain offering" (9:27).

Then for three and a half years, the Antichrist will defile the temple by erecting an idol and making Israel worship him as their god.[18] Nevertheless, at the end of these three and a half years, the "one that is decreed"—Christ—will come and pour "out [judgment] on the one [the Antichrist] who makes desolate" (9:27).

Christ's second coming will bring an end to the "one week," or tribulation, foretold in Daniel. And at the end of the "week," the glorious promises of forgiveness and righteousness given in Daniel 9:24 will wash over the nation of Israel and it will be what it should be, "the ransomed of the Lord . . . [full of] everlasting joy" (Isaiah 51:11).

STARTING YOUR JOURNEY

How easy it is for us to get lost in the minutiae of the numbers! But while these numbers and the events associated with them are important to understanding Israel's history and future, two ideas add up, especially for those of us who live in the gap between the sixty-ninth and the seventieth weeks.

First, *God deals in specifics—He's a God of details*. Jeremiah's prophecy regarding seventy years of exile was exact in its fulfillment. Daniel's vision of the succession of world empires is documented historically. And the fulfillment of Gabriel's words to Daniel regarding the timing of Christ's arrival in Jerusalem is utterly astounding.

Take a look at some of the messianic prophecies in the Old Testament, then read of their fulfillment in the person and work of Jesus Christ as chronicled in the New Testament. Fill in the chart below:

Old Testament	New Testament	Fulfilled Prophecy
Isaiah 7:14	Matthew 1:18–25	
Micah 5:2	Matthew 2:1	
Isaiah 35:5	Matthew 9:35	
Zechariah 9:9	Matthew 21:1–11	
Isaiah 53:5	John 19:34	
Isaiah 53:7	Matthew 27:12	
Psalm 22:18	Matthew 27:35	
Isaiah 53:9	Matthew 27:57–60	

Second, *God keeps His promises—He's a God of integrity*. God can be taken at His word. He is who He says He is and He does what He says He will do.

When you look at the prophecies and their fulfillment in the chart on the previous page, what is your first reaction?

____

____

____

Does this knowledge impact how you view God? His Word? Explain.

____

____

____

The greatest truths are sometimes the simplest—one plus one equals two. But at other times, important truth doesn't come all that easily; understanding it requires much more of us—think of $E = MC^2$. The danger, of course, in trying to figure out these deeper truths is being confused by the numbers. They can seem so complicated!

As we added and multiplied a lot of numbers important to Israel's history and future and looked at God's fulfillment of prophecy, at least two items should have become very clear: God is sovereign over even the smallest details, and He is completely trustworthy.

Now that's arithmetic we all can appreciate!

LESSON SIX

SUPERNATURAL PHENOMENA BETWEEN HEAVEN AND EARTH

Daniel 10

THE HEART OF THE MATTER

Skeptics say, "I won't believe in anything I can't see or touch." "Prove it," is their watchword. But many unexplainable things happen on earth. Christians call them "miracles." Skeptics call them "coincidences." Is it possible that, through their sophisticated élan, skeptics are rejecting their own intuitive knowledge of things unseen? The ancients were comfortable with the concept that reality exists in two worlds—the physical and the spiritual. Today most people sneer at such notions, dismissing them as mythology.

Daniel understood that two realms existed. And biblical truth compels us to stand with Daniel and the ancients. From their vantage point, we'll "see" the reality of the unseen, and that new perspective will transform our understanding of prayer.

DISCOVERING THE WAY

Noted atheist and satirist H. L. Mencken was a skeptic extraordinaire. But this didn't prevent him from breaking with the spirit of his age and recognizing the truth—if not spiritually, at least socially and economically—that the phenomenon of the intangible is very real. In his journal, *Minority Report*, Mencken wrote, "Penetrating so many secrets, we cease to believe in the unknowable. But there it sits nevertheless, calmly licking its chops."[1]

That something is unknowable does not make it unreal or unbelievable. Daniel understood this truth. He had spent a lifetime engulfed in mystery—dreams and visions, angelic visitations, and divine deliverances. So when another angel stepped out of the unseen world, Daniel knew the unknown was not only sitting on the edge of heaven but also actively intervening in his life.

Why do you think people in our society have ceased to believe in things that can't be proven? What are some of their reasons for not believing in the spiritual realm?

Can you give any evidence for or against the existence of a spiritual realm from your life experiences? Please share.

What does the Bible say about the unseen world in Ephesians 6:12?

BACKGROUND AND SETTING

In chapter 9, Daniel was engaged in concentrated prayer when Gabriel arrived and explained to him the mystery of the seventy "sevens." Chapter 10 finds Daniel a few years older and once again in intense prayer . . . for three long weeks.

Read Daniel 10:1–3.

A momentous event had recently occurred for Israel. When Daniel read in Jeremiah's scroll that "the desolations of Jerusalem" would last for "seventy years" (Daniel 9:2), the year was 538 BC. However, by "the third year of Cyrus king of Persia" (10:1), the calendar had rolled to 536 BC.[2] By this time, Jeremiah's prophecy had been fulfilled. Cyrus had issued a decree sometime during the first year of his reign that allowed the Jews to return to Jerusalem and begin reconstructing God's temple (Ezra 1:1–4).[3]

Now in his eighties, Daniel remained behind in Babylon and received a revelation "of great conflict" (Daniel 10:1). We aren't given much information about the content of this vision. Daniel simply wrote that it "concerned a great war" (10:1 NIV).

Even though the exile had ended and God's promises of restoration were being fulfilled, Daniel's vision of future trouble for Israel brought him to his knees in mourning and fasting for three weeks (10:2–3). Only eating what was necessary, he refused any pleasant food or drink. And in keeping with mourning, he used no ointment to wash and perfume his body.

MESSENGER AND VISION

For three weeks—twenty-one days—Daniel prayed and received no answer. Three weeks of bland foods, of bending aching and creaking knees, of weeping sorrowful tears, of crying out to God. And still, no answer . . . until a special delivery came by an unexpected and unforeseen visitor.

Read Daniel 10:4–9.

Daniel was standing by the Tigris River, perhaps on governmental business, when suddenly he saw a "man dressed in linen, whose waist was girded with a belt of pure gold of Uphaz" (Daniel 10:5). But he wasn't just an ordinary man dressed in a rich, finely tailored suit. His body shone like a precious jewel, the radiance of his face flashed like lightning against a dark sky, his eyes burned with intensity, his arms and feet were like mirrored bronze, and his voice sounded like a thousand voices (10:6).[4]

Angels appear at various times throughout Scripture. In the following verses, what do these angels look like?

Isaiah 6:1–4

____

____

Ezekiel 10:9–17

____

____

Luke 24:4–5

____

____

Seeing nothing and perhaps hearing nothing, Daniel's companions were nevertheless struck by sudden terror. Running in fear, they hid themselves and left Daniel to face this mysterious presence alone (Daniel 10:7–8). Standing before this one from the supernatural world, Daniel "went weak in the knees, the blood drained from [his] face. . . . At the sound of [the angel's voice, Daniel] fainted, fell flat on the ground, face in the dirt" (10:8–9 MSG).

Place yourself in Daniel's sandals. How do you think you would have responded to the vision of this angel?

____

____

____

____

PRAYER AND RESPONSE

When we pray, our words leave the realm of the physical and enter the realm of the spiritual. However, sometimes we feel like our prayers never penetrate the ceiling. Daniel's three weeks of prayer must have been one of those times. But now, with his face in the dirt, Daniel was about to hear just how effective his prayers had been. As we eavesdrop on the conversation between the angel and Daniel, five principles regarding prayer will emerge.

 **Read Daniel 10:10–21.**

Reaching down, the angel touched Daniel and helped him up from his knees, telling him to "stand upright" (Daniel 10:10–11). Addressing Daniel as a "man of high esteem" (10:11), as Gabriel had previously (9:23), the angel said he had been sent to help Daniel understand what would happen in the future (10:11).

The angel encouraged Daniel by telling him that from the *very moment* Daniel humbled himself and prayed for understanding of what the future held for his people, God heard and hurried the angel along to deliver an answer (10:12).

This truth leads to the first principle of prayer: *When a believer prays, he or she is immediately heard by God.* The distance from our mouths to God's ear is like the length of a flea's whisker. Any day at any time, we have immediate and open access to the throne room of God—and He's never too busy for His children.

Read each of the following passages, and write down the promise in each one.

Isaiah 30:19

____

____

Isaiah 65:24

____

____

Matthew 6:8

____

____

If God hears our prayers immediately, then why do we often have to wait a long time for an answer? Why did Daniel have to wait three weeks?

The angel said to Daniel, "I was waylaid by the angel-prince of the kingdom of Persia and was delayed for a good three weeks. But then Michael, one of the chief angel-princes, intervened to help me" (Daniel 10:13 MSG).

For twenty-one days a heavenly wrestling match had ensued, pitting God's holy angel against Satan's "prince of the kingdom of Persia," a demon who had been dispatched to prevent the angel from delivering God's answer to Daniel.[5]

Notice the second principle of prayer: *Demonic forces can delay answers to prayer*. How common is this? It's hard to say, but Scripture clearly teaches that Satan is our enemy and seeks to hinder our communion with God.

How does 1 Peter 5:8 describe the Devil and his purpose?

How do you think the Devil accomplishes his designs (see 1 John 2:15–16 for a clue)?

Read Ephesians 6:10–18, and answer the following questions.

How does Paul instruct believers to engage in spiritual battle (6:10–11, 18)?

What six things are we to "put on," specifically?

1.	2.
3.	4.
5.	6.

How can you apply Paul's words in your everyday life?

DIGGING DEEPER
Why Aren't My Prayers Answered?

Daniel 10 provides one reason why prayers may be delayed, but this is not the sole reason why answers to our prayers are delayed or even remain unanswered. Henry W. Holloman offers seven requirements for praying according to God's will, the foundation of all godly prayer:

- Praying from a pure heart (Psalm 66:18)
- Praying in faith (James 1:5–8)
- Praying in obedience (1 John 3:22)
- Praying while abiding in Christ (John 15:7)
- Praying to glorify God (1 Corinthians 10:31)
- Praying in order to mature in Christ (2 Peter 3:18)
- Praying in the Holy Spirit (Ephesians 6:18)[6]

If you are struggling with an unanswered prayer, examine your heart and motives according to the list above. If all is well, continue to be patient and trust that God will answer in His perfect time (Psalm 4:3; 66:19–20).

After three weeks of this cosmic struggle, the archangel Michael came to the assistance of God's messenger angel and he was freed from the grip of the demonic prince of Persia.[7]

When the angel reached Daniel, he described his battle and then repeated that he had come to help Daniel understand what would befall Israel in the "latter days, for the vision [of great conflict (Daniel 10:1)] pertains to the days yet future" (10:14).

Daniel stood, mouth agape and staring at the ground (Daniel 10:15). His prayer had shaken the abode of Satan and unleashed a demon from the pit of hell. And now, sensing that the answer to his prayer was ominous, Daniel was completely dumb-struck. Touched again by the angel, this time on the lips, Daniel confessed that the vision of the angelic appearance and of what awaited Israel had caused him great sorrow and left him weary, weak, and breathless (10:16–17).

In Daniel's response, we see the third principle of prayer: *Wrestling in prayer is exhausting work*. Prayer is not for the weak-willed but for the tenacious.

Daniel wrestled in prayer for three weeks. Have you ever spent anguished moments or hours in prayer for something or someone? Describe your experience. What did you learn from this time in prayer?

God's angels are ministering spirits, and this one ministered to Daniel. Placing his hand on the aged prophet, the angel affirmed Daniel's worth before God and gave him the message of *shalom*—peace—and courage (10:18–19). At the angel's words, "courage surged up within [Daniel]" (10:19 MSG)—he was now ready to hear God's answer to his prayers.

That takes us to the fourth principle of prayer: *Following such exhausting experiences, extra measures of strength return*. God's timing is perfect—He is never late, never early—and He brings encouragement just when we need it.

God's creativity is unlimited. He can strengthen us in myriad ways—through people, events, His Word, and even through angels when we're not even aware of it (Hebrew 13:2). Has God encouraged you after a spiritual battle? How?

Meeting this angel with his unbelievable but very real story of spiritual hand-to-hand combat was enough to leave anyone's head spinning. So the angel specifically asked Daniel whether or not he understood the angel's mission. He had come to deliver God's message, but afterward he must return to the battle and reengage the prince of Persia. Later, he said that another would come, the "prince of Greece" (Daniel 10:20). No one stood against these demon-princes, save Michael, an angelic protector of Israel, and this angel (10:21).

The angel's words reveal the fifth principle of prayer: *Overcoming demonic forces is not a once-and-for-all matter.*

When engaged in a spiritual battle, the promise in 1 John 4:4 should encourage you to persevere. Read this verse, and write it in your own words.

Before leaving, the angel promised to tell Daniel "what is inscribed in the writing of truth" (Daniel 10:21)[8]—of Israel's future under Persian rule (11:2–4), under Greek rule (11:5–35), during the tribulation (11:36–45), and in the millennial kingdom (12:1 –3).

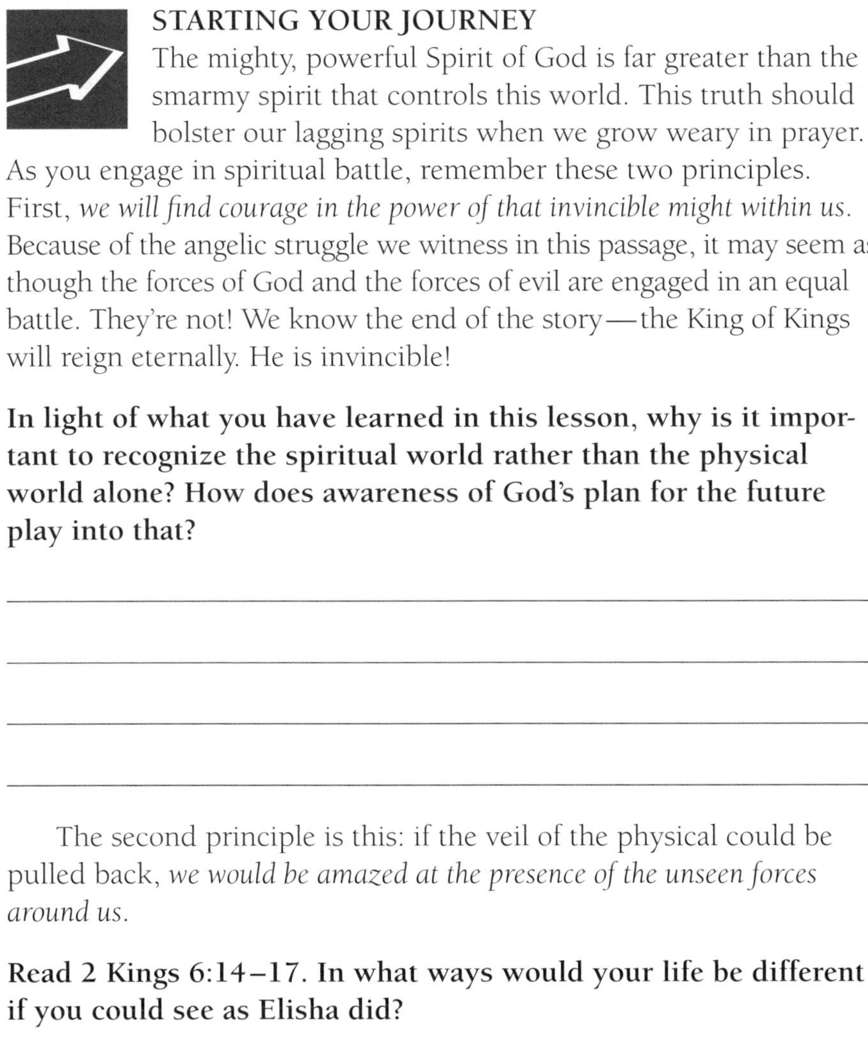

STARTING YOUR JOURNEY

The mighty, powerful Spirit of God is far greater than the smarmy spirit that controls this world. This truth should bolster our lagging spirits when we grow weary in prayer. As you engage in spiritual battle, remember these two principles. First, *we will find courage in the power of that invincible might within us*. Because of the angelic struggle we witness in this passage, it may seem as though the forces of God and the forces of evil are engaged in an equal battle. They're not! We know the end of the story—the King of Kings will reign eternally. He is invincible!

In light of what you have learned in this lesson, why is it important to recognize the spiritual world rather than the physical world alone? How does awareness of God's plan for the future play into that?

The second principle is this: if the veil of the physical could be pulled back, *we would be amazed at the presence of the unseen forces around us*.

Read 2 Kings 6:14–17. In what ways would your life be different if you could see as Elisha did?

Skeptics may scoff, but the Bible makes it clear that there is more to the world than meets the eye. God's holy angels surround us, ready to fight valiantly on our behalf. Let us do battle, therefore, on our knees, armed with spiritual weapons. And let us not shirk our duty, even if it costs us anguish for days, because the souls of men and women are the victor's prize.

LESSON SEVEN

WARS AND RUMORS OF WAR

Daniel 11:1—12:1

THE HEART OF THE MATTER

In his vision, Daniel witnessed the cruel spectacle of war. He observed the battles that would take place between the successors of Alexander the Great as well as the future climactic and demonic warfare at the time of the Antichrist. As we study Daniel's vision, we'll see a grim picture of the inescapable worldwide war that will surround those who will enter the tribulation without Christ—unless we tell them about the Prince of Peace.

DISCOVERING THE WAY

After the fog of war cleared, revealing the full extent of the carnage of World War II, President Harry S. Truman, at the signing of the United Nations Charter, naively declared,

> [This Charter] is a declaration of great faith by the nations of the earth—faith that war is not inevitable, faith that peace can be maintained. If we had had this Charter a few years ago—and above all, the will to use it—millions now dead would be alive. If we should falter in the future in our will to use it, millions now living will surely die.[1]

Unfortunately, humanity has yet to learn the wisdom history has to teach—that wars are not fought because we lack the will to seek peace; wars are fought because we lack the character to exercise that will. Our desire and efforts to end war forever are futile, as history attests.

What does James 4:1–2 teach us about the causes of war?

____

____

____

In our long, bloodstained history, we should have learned by now that as long as humans direct our affairs, war is inevitable. This lesson will come to fruition when the rotten fruit of war ripens in the end times.

WARS: THE UGLY FACTS OF THE PAST

Jesus's disciples believed that they lived on the verge of a new Jewish kingdom, a time when Jesus would reign as King. They asked Jesus to pin down exactly when the "end of the age" would come, but instead Jesus warned them to look out for false messiahs and not to be alarmed about "wars and rumors of wars" in the future (Matthew 24:3–6). From that time until now, the end has not yet come, but wars and rumors of wars remain constant.

The study of human history is the study of war.

Describe what war looks like, based on your own experiences.

____

____

____

Do you think war is inevitable? Why, or why not?

____

____

____

WARS: THE ULTIMATE CAMPAIGNS OF THE FUTURE

Daniel 11 is one of the most remarkable chapters in the entire Bible. Donald Campbell states, "In the first 35 verses there are at least 135 prophecies that have been literally fulfilled and can be corroborated by a study of the history of the period."[2]

Read Daniel 11:1–2.

Having wrenched loose from the grip of the "prince of Persia," God's messenger began to reveal to Daniel the details of wars to come; wars that would be simply skirmishes in comparison to the climactic war of the last days.

The angel informed Daniel that "in the first year of Darius the Mede" he had begun to aid Darius and protect him from harm (Daniel 11:1). This information indicates that this messenger was probably Gabriel—the angel who had interpreted the vision of the seventy "sevens" for Daniel (see 9:1, 21).

Gabriel told Daniel that four other kings would "arise in Persia" (11:2).[3] The fourth king, whom we know as Xerxes I, would grow in power and wealth and would invade Greece.[4]

Read Daniel 11:3–4.

Alexander the Great was the "mighty king" who Gabriel said would "rule with great authority and do as he pleases" (11:3). Like a meteor against the night sky, Alexander burned brightly and then was gone. His kingdom was divided not among his heirs or according to his wishes but among his four generals (11:4).[5]

Gabriel next drew Daniel's attention to two generals, "the king of the South" and the "king of the North," and the wars between them. The kingdom of the South was ruled by the Ptolemies, who took Egypt as their possession after the death of Alexander. The kingdom of the North was ruled by the Seleucids, who reigned in Syria. The battleground in between the two kingdoms was Israel. Surveying almost 150 years of Egyptian and Syrian warfare under these kingdoms, Gabriel's specific details and their exact fulfillment have astounded historians for centuries.[6]

Founding the Dynasties

Read Daniel 11:5–6.

Foretold in Daniel 11:5, the first "king of the South" was Ptolemy I Soter (323–285 BC). The prince "who will gain ascendancy over him and obtain dominion" (Daniel 11:5) was the first Seleucid "king of the North" (11:6), Seleucus I Nicator (312–281 BC). Ruling from Babylon, Seleucus I came under attack from another of Alexander's generals. Seeking the help of Ptolemy I, Seleucus defeated the other general in 312 BC and established a great empire.

When Ptolemy I died, his son Ptolemy II Philadelphus ruled in Egypt (285–246 BC). After Seleucus I was murdered in 281 BC and after the reign of his successor,[7] Antiochus II Theos came to the Syrian throne (262–246 BC). Though they were bitter enemies, Ptolemy II and Antiochus II formed an alliance when Ptolemy's daughter, Berenice, married Antiochus II. The marriage came to a tragic end when Laodice, the powerful woman whom Antiochus divorced in order to marry Berenice, poisoned Antiochus, Berenice, and their infant son. Notice the exact fulfillment of Gabriel's words in Daniel 11:6 regarding the "daughter of the king of the South" and her untimely demise.

War between the Dynasties

Read Daniel 11:7–9.

Laodice established her son, Seleucus II Callinicus (246–227 BC), as the "king of the North" after the death of Antiochus II. Ptolemy III Euergetes (246–221 BC), now the "king of the South" and the brother of Berenice, sought vengeance against his sister's murderer. Invading and "enter[ing] the fortress of the king of the North,"

Ptolemy succeeded in defeating Seleucus and putting Laodice to death. Satisfied, Ptolemy took great amounts of treasure back to Egypt and ceased his northern advance, just as Gabriel had predicted in Daniel 11:7–8.

Stinging from defeat, Seleucus II invaded Egypt but was quickly overcome and had to "return to his own land" of Syria (see Daniel 11:9).

Antiochus III the Great

Read Daniel 11:10–12.

The "sons" mentioned in Daniel 11:10 were Seleucus III Soter and Antiochus III the Great. Seleucus III came to the throne (227–223 BC) at the death of his father but was murdered while on a military campaign. In his place, Antiochus III ascended the throne of Syria (223–187 BC).

Antiochus III was successful in pushing the Egyptians back to the southern border of Israel (Daniel 11:10), but in 217 BC he was defeated when Ptolemy IV Philopator (221–204 BC), the "king of the South," became "enraged" and met him on the field at Raphia. Gabriel's prophecy in Daniel 11:11–12 was fulfilled to the smallest detail when Antiochus III and his "great multitude" faced the larger force of Ptolemy IV and lost "tens of thousands" to the Egyptians.

Read Daniel 11:13–16.

Antiochus's defeat was bitter, but he rebuilt his army. And "after an interval of some years" (11:13)—years that included the mysterious death of Ptolemy IV and the crowning of 6-year-old Ptolemy V—Antiochus III pressed his advantage against Egypt. Forming an alliance with Philip V of Macedonia and enlisting Jewish soldiers as foretold in 11:14, Antiochus III defeated Ptolemy V's General Scopas at Paneas and captured the "well-fortified city" of Sidon (11:15). The "Beautiful Land" of Israel was now under Seleucid control (11:16). Each and every one of the incredibly detailed predictions recorded by Daniel continued to unfold in history.

Read Daniel 11:17–20.

Years later, Antiochus III gave his daughter, Cleopatra I,[8] in marriage to Ptolemy V as a sign of peace, hoping she would deliver Egypt into his hands. However, she refused to betray her husband (reflected in Daniel 11:17).

"Turn[ing] his face to the coastlands" of Asia Minor and Greece (11:18), Antiochus III then marched westward. He was met by Commander Lucius Cornelius Scipio, the Roman general who had defeated him at Thermopylae in 191 BC and at Magnesia in 190–189 BC. Disgraced again, Antiochus "turn[ed] his face toward the fortresses of his own land" (11:19). But before reaching Syria, he died while attempting to plunder the temple of Bel at Elam in order to pay his tribute to Rome.

Seleucus IV Philopator (187–176 BC), Antiochus's son, was left with the heavy debt to Rome, so he sent tax collectors throughout the "Jewel of his kingdom" (11:20). Heliodorus, his treasurer, went to Jerusalem and attempted to plunder the temple. Soon after, Seleucus IV died mysteriously, possibly poisoned by Heliodorus. Just as Daniel 11:20 predicted, this king died, "though not in anger nor in battle."

Antiochus IV Epiphanes

Read Daniel 11:21–35.

We met this "despicable person" (11:21) in a previous lesson. His name was Antiochus IV Epiphanes.[9]

Skim pages 28–30 in lesson 3. Then write a summary of what you have learned so far about Antiochus Epiphanes.

____

____

____

____

Antiochus IV Epiphanes was a pivotal person in the history of Israel. Through deceptive means, he stole the kingdom from his nephew and rightful heir, Demetrius Soter, fulfilling Daniel 11:21. Successfully defending his territory against an attack by the Egyptian army, he secured his hold on Syria and the surrounding area. His despicable treatment of the Jews began when he had the pious and respected high priest Onias III, "the prince of the covenant" (Daniel 11:22), murdered and replaced him with his own priest.[10]

Winning military victories and making alliances only to break them, Antiochus's power grew (fulfilling 11:23). And then, in a shrewd political maneuver, Antiochus "accomplish[ed] what his fathers never did" (11:24), winning the support of the people by redistributing the kingdom's wealth.

When Antiochus grew in "strength and courage" (11:25), he decided to attack Egypt, marching against "the king of the South," Ptolemy VI Philometer (180–145 BC). They met on the coastal road of Gaza.[11] Egypt was defeated because of the treasonous acts of Ptolemy's advisors, just as Gabriel had predicted (11:25–26).

Meeting Antiochus IV at Memphis, Ptolemy VI sought a peace agreement. But both men fully intended to deceive each other, so they failed to reach a binding treaty (fulfilling 11:27). Antiochus, as the victor, left with "much plunder," but he was very frustrated that he couldn't completely conquer Egypt. So he took out his anger on the Jews, the people of the "holy covenant" (11:28). He desecrated the temple at Jerusalem on the way back to Syria.

Two years later, Antiochus IV Epiphanes set out to conquer Egypt again (as predicted in Daniel 11:29). This time he was met by the Romans and unceremoniously turned away.[12] Antiochus was utterly humiliated, and he again vented his frustration on the Jews. Antiochus sent his men to desecrate the Jerusalem temple a second time, abolishing the ritual of daily sacrifice and setting up the "abomination of desolation." In a flagrant act of rebellion and hatred, Antiochus erected an altar to Zeus in the temple and sacrificed a pig. Then he required the Jews to abandon their covenant with God and worship the idol—or face horrendous persecution. Here again, Gabriel's prophecy was fulfilled even to the smallest detail (see Daniel 11:30–32).

The activities of Antiochus IV Epiphanes detailed in Daniel 11:29–32 mirror the description of him in Daniel 8:9–12. Compare the two by filling out the chart with the historical data provided in this chapter.

Prophecies		Fulfillment in History
11:29	8:9	
11:30	8:9	
11:31	8:10–12	
11:32	8:12	

Not everyone would be beguiled or forced into worshiping Antiochus's idol. A small band of "people who [knew] their God" took action against Antiochus (as predicted in 11:32). This rebellion by the priestly family of Mattathias and his five sons, known as the Maccabean revolt, began with a few followers, but as Gabriel promised, the movement grew in spite of intense persecution and eventually triumphed (11:33–35).[13]

Antiochus IV Epiphanes was future to Daniel and is history to us. But the next section of prophecy Daniel recorded is still future. It speaks of the Antichrist, the person who will come in the manner of Antiochus IV Epiphanes. We've already had the misfortune of being introduced to this loathsome person, but in the next set of verses, we'll learn a little more about this demonic individual who will arise in the last days.

The Antichrist

Skim back over lesson 2 and summarize what you know about the Antichrist.

____

____

____

____

____

 **Read Daniel 11:36–12:1.**

The Antichrist will make a peace treaty with Israel but will break it after three and a half years (see Daniel 9:27). At that time he will establish himself as an object of worship in the Jewish temple. This prophecy in Daniel 11:36 is echoed in 2 Thessalonians 2:3–4 and Revelation 13:4–8.

The Antichrist will be proud and self-willed, exalting himself above every god (see Daniel 11:37). He will despise women[14] and will honor warfare, pouring out the treasure of his kingdom to advance his military goals and rewarding those who follow him (11:37–39). His success as a political, military, and religious leader will come with the aid of "a foreign god," Satan (11:39).

Subjugated under the Antichrist's authority, nations will grow dissatisfied and rebel "at the end time" (11:40). In a two-pronged attack, the kingdoms of the South and the North[15] will march in military array against the Antichrist, who will pour over countries like a torrential flood to meet these armies in the "Beautiful Land" of Israel (11:40–41).[16]

Initially victorious, the Antichrist will pursue his enemies through Egypt, plundering the country's treasures, and then continue his pursuit into Libya and Ethiopia (11:42–43). Pressing his advantage in the South, the Antichrist will hear disturbing rumors of armies from the East (see related prophecies in Revelation 9:16–19; 16:12) and the North amassing against him. In a fit of rage, he will annihilate these invaders (Daniel 11:44).

Reasserting his authority, the Antichrist will set up his capital in Jerusalem—"the beautiful Holy Mountain" (11:45). But the reign of this despot will certainly come to an ignominious end; "no one will help him" (Daniel 11:45; see also Revelation 19:19–21).

All of this will certainly come to pass, including "a time of distress such as never occurred." What about Israel? Daniel must have wondered. Gabriel assured him that while individual Jews will die during the terrible time of the tribulation, the angel Michael, protector of Israel, will intervene and prevent the Antichrist from exterminating the Jewish people (Daniel 12:1).[17]

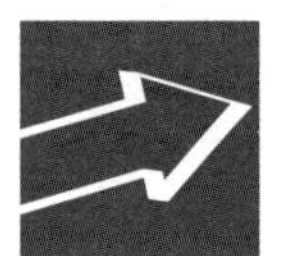

STARTING YOUR JOURNEY

Whew! We covered a lot of historical and prophetic ground! So, what are we supposed to do with all this information? Take a few minutes to answer the following questions.

Read 2 Peter 3:3–9. What is the warning in verses 3 and 4?

____

____

Paraphrase the description given in verses 5–7.

____

____

What is the promise contained in verses 8 and 9?

____

____

Knowing that the Lord wishes for "all to come to repentance," how can you participate in His goal? (For help, see Matthew 28:19–20 and Acts 1:8.)

___

___

___

Because Christ is coming back to rapture His church—an event that could happen at any moment—and because God's judgment, including horrific worldwide warfare, is assured, we should be about the business of telling others how they can escape the end of the world.

So who will you tell about the Prince of Peace?

"Mankind must put an end to war—or war will put an end to mankind," John F. Kennedy announced to the United Nations.[18] However, our desire and work to end war is futile, as history attests. Scripture is clear—war will only end when Christ returns to rule the world in justice and righteousness. If we who follow the Prince of Peace falter in our task to tell others about Christ, millions now living will surely die.

LESSON EIGHT

A PROPHETIC QUARTET

Daniel 12:1–4

THE HEART OF THE MATTER

Life lived under the sun can have a depressing quality, or at least Solomon thought so. "Vanity of vanities! All is vanity," he said. "The living know they will die; but the dead do not know anything, nor have they any longer a reward, for their memory is forgotten" (Ecclesiastes 1:2; 9:5). Live, die, and disappear from memory—that's encouragement for you!

But is this life all there is? Do we live in vain? Daniel, as he comes to the close of his book, received a vision of four groups of people whose lives and deaths answer with an unequivocal *no*; all is *not* vanity. These four groups who live in the future will have significant lives that will echo in eternity—never to be forgotten by God.

DISCOVERING THE WAY

We wake up every morning and hear about a newly famous person. He or she was anonymous the night before, but today this person's face and name are splashed all over television, radio, magazines, and the Internet. But fame is fickle and fleeting. Those who are famous will surely fade from memory as quickly as the morning fog dissolves in the heat of the sun. Writer H. L. Mencken summed it up well:

> When I hear a man applauded by the mob I always feel a pang of pity for him. All he has to do to be hissed is to live long enough. . . . The mob is faithful only in its infidelity. It always stones those it has worshipped.[1]

The yearning for fame is a powerful inducement. American statesman Alexander Hamilton understood this motivation: "The love of fame, the ruling passion of the noblest minds . . . [will] prompt a man to plan and undertake extensive and arduous enterprises."[2]

After observing the celebrities in our culture, brainstorm five or more characteristics that define their lives.

____

____

____

Have you ever wanted to be famous? Why, or why not?

____

____

____

Daniel was a famous man, though he never sought to be one. For him, fame wasn't important—faithfulness was. As he continued to wrestle with Gabriel's explanation of the future, he must have derived some encouragement from the realization that, whether or not the world recognizes what we do, God never forgets the service of His people.

SETTING AND BACKGROUND

Following his descriptions of the wars that will lead up to the climactic battle between Christ and the Antichrist, Gabriel assured Daniel that even when hell breaks loose on the earth, God will send the archangel Michael to protect a remnant of the Jewish people. This terrible time yet future is the three and a half years known as the great tribulation. Its horrors will be unprecedented in the annals of Israel's history or human history (Daniel 12:1).

Read Revelation 13:5–8, and describe the activities of the Antichrist during the great tribulation.

____

____

____

____

Read Revelation 13:11–17, and list the activities of the False Prophet during the great tribulation.

____

____

____

____

What can we glean from Revelation 7:1–8 and 14:1 about the Antichrist's ability to exterminate the Jewish people?

____

____

____

____

PEOPLE AND EVENTS

The nation of Israel will survive the great tribulation, but Gabriel didn't promise that individual Jews would not die—they will. Countless people will be martyred, "from every nation and all tribes and peoples and tongues," including Jews who have come to faith in Christ since the beginning of the tribulation (Revelation 7:9–17).

Read Daniel 12:1–3.

God keeps meticulous records, not just about those who have gone before us but also regarding those who will come after us, including the four groups of people in this passage.

Those Written in the Book

The Bible is filled with references to God's "books."[3] We've already studied two types of these books—the books of judgment (Daniel 7:10) and the Book of Truth (10:21). So what book was Gabriel talking about in Daniel 12:1?

This book is most likely "the book of life" that is described in Revelation 20:12, 15. Those who begin a personal relationship with Jesus Christ during the current church age will be rescued from the tribulation (1 Thessalonians 4:15–17; Revelation 3:10). Those who come to faith in Christ after the rapture—Jews and Gentiles alike—will have to endure this terrible time, and many will die. But in the end, all who know Jesus Christ as Savior will have their names written in the Book of Life—and they will receive the eternal reward of living with Him in perfect peace (Revelation 21:1–7).

Once the tribulation has come to a close, and after the thousand years of Christ's reign on earth (the millennial kingdom) is complete, Satan will be punished. Then there will come a time of great judgment. Sitting upon a white throne, Christ will open the Book of Life, along with books of judgment that contain every person's deeds. Every person whose name is not found in the Book of Life will be judged and receive the just rewards of his or her deeds—eternal damnation in the lake of fire (Revelation 20:11–15).

Is your name written in the Book of Life? If you're not sure, please read "How to Begin a Relationship with God" at the back of this Bible Companion.

Those Who Die during the Tribulation

What will happen to those who die—believers and unbelievers—during the tribulation? Gabriel told Daniel that "those who sleep in the dust" will be resurrected (Daniel 12:2). The idea of resurrection, of the rejoining of spirit with a renewed body, is uniquely biblical and mysterious. The Bible describes four different kinds of resurrections.[4]

The resurrection of Christ was the first (Matthew 28:6; 1 Corinthians 15:22–23). The second resurrection will occur at the rapture, when those believers who die during the church age will come forth from their graves and join with Christians who are alive to meet Jesus in the air (John 14:1–3; 1 Corinthians 15:51–54; 1 Thessalonians 4:13–17). The third resurrection is described in Daniel 12:2 and deals with those who will be awakened to "everlasting life." This resurrection will take place after the tribulation at the second coming of Christ when all Old Testament and tribulation saints will be raised (Isaiah 26:19; Revelation 7:13–17; 20:4).[5] The fourth resurrection will be delayed a thousand years while Christ reigns as King in the millennial kingdom (Revelation 20:5), but when it happens, it will include all unbelievers from the beginning of time. This is the resurrection unto "disgrace and everlasting contempt" (Daniel 12:2; see also Revelation 20:12–15). The following chart provides a comprehensive overview of these resurrections.

WHAT HAPPENS TO A PERSON AFTER DEATH?

"And inasmuch as it is appointed for men to die once and after this comes judgment." (Hebrews 9:27)

	At Death	Bodily Resurrection	Judgment	Eternal Destination
Christian	Christ's Presence Soul / Body The Grave	Resurrection at the Rapture	Judgment Seat of Christ in Heaven for Rewards	Heaven
Old Testament Believer	Paradise/ Abraham's Bosom Soul / Body The Grave	Resurrection at Christ's Second Coming	Judgment on Earth for Rewards	Heaven
Tribulation Believer	Christ's Presence Soul / Body The Grave	Resurrection at Christ's Second Coming	Judgment on Earth for Rewards	Heaven
Unbeliever	Sheol/Hades Torment Soul / Body The Grave	Resurrection at the End of the Millennium	Judgment at the Great White Throne for Sins	Hell/ Gehenna/ Lake of Fire

Those Who Have Insight

During the great tribulation, many will worship the Antichrist and take his number (Revelation 13:8, 15–18). But others will see through his deceptions and teach the truth, even though it will cost some of them their lives (Daniel 11:33, 35). These new believers are those to whom God will give "insight" (12:3), an understanding of His Word and the context in which they are living. Wisely, they will teach the Scriptures and give testimony about the death and resurrection of Christ in order to encourage fellow believers in the midst of terrible suffering.

These wise ones will not be forgotten by God. Their reward will be to shine as brightly as the heavens, reflecting God's own glory (Psalm 19:1).

Those Who Lead the Many to Righteousness

Daniel 12:3 also introduces us to a fourth group of people—tribulation evangelists. These courageous believers will risk everything to lead others to Christ. Many will be martyred for their faith (Revelation 6:9–11; 13:10), but their very willingness to die for the truth will inspire some to seek Jesus.

Though the world will heartlessly discard them, God will not forget them (see 1 Corinthians 15:58). To Him, they will be "like the stars forever and ever" (Daniel 12:3).

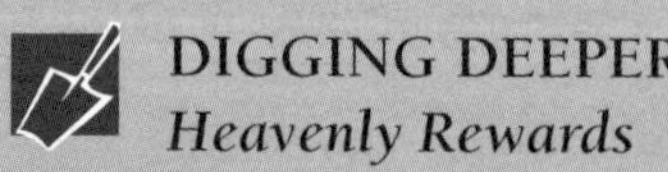

DIGGING DEEPER
Heavenly Rewards

The Bible often speaks of heavenly rewards for God's faithful ones, especially in the New Testament. Scripture's usual metaphor for rewards is "crowns." The Greek word used is *stephanos*—a laurel wreath awarded to the winner in an athletic game.[6] At least five direct biblical references describe crowns that are available to the faithful.

1. *An imperishable crown* for those who lead a disciplined life (1 Corinthians 9:25)
2. *A crown of rejoicing* for those who evangelize and disciple others (1 Thessalonians 2:19)
3. *A crown of righteousness* for those who long for the Lord's appearing (2 Timothy 4:8)
4. *A crown of life* for those who endure trials and persecution (James 1:12; Revelation 2:10)
5. *A crown of glory* for those who shepherd God's people faithfully (1 Peter 5:1–4)

Like an Olympian standing on the victor's podium, so faithful followers of Christ will one day receive a reward from His hand (see Revelation 22:12).

WORDS AND KNOWLEDGE

Beginning in chapter 10, Gabriel took Daniel on a trip from 536 BC to the very end of time, describing the future. Now addressing Daniel personally, Gabriel gave him a set of specific instructions.

Read Daniel 12:4.

Daniel was charged to keep all of the events that had happened in his life and the visions he had seen intact in a book—concealed and sealed up. Daniel could not understand all the prophecies (Daniel 12:8), but nevertheless his book would be preserved until the "end of time."

Gabriel promised that during the tribulation, men and women will rush "back and forth" looking for answers to what is happening in the world. Though "knowledge will increase," their search for answers will be futile until they discover God's Word. The book of Daniel, along with John's Revelation, will provide those who come to believe during the tribulation—Jews and Gentiles—with encouragement that the end is near and that Christ will reward them for their faithfulness.

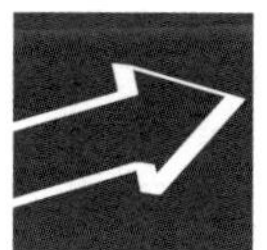

STARTING YOUR JOURNEY

After having studied Daniel's visions, we can affirm anew God's testimony about Himself:

> "My thoughts are not your thoughts,
> Nor are your ways My ways. . . .
> For as the heavens are higher than the earth,
> So are My ways higher than your ways
> And My thoughts than your thoughts."
> (Isaiah 55:8–9)

We've been struggling to comprehend God's thoughts and ways throughout the book of Daniel. When we acknowledge that His ways and thoughts are higher than ours, we can also claim these three truths.

First, *we honor the famous and soon forget them, but God honors the unknown and never forgets them.*

Read Ecclesiastes 1:11 and 9:5. Do you think Solomon was correct—that everything and everyone that have come before, even the dead, are soon forgotten? Why, or why not?

What does 1 Samuel 16:7 say about the way God sees things as opposed to the way we see them?

What promise do you find in Hebrews 6:10? In what ways does this passage encourage you?

Second, *we give earthly rewards, but God gives heavenly rewards.*

Have you ever won an award? If so, what was it for? What did it mean to you at the time? What does that award mean to you today? Where is it?

What is the fundamental difference between earthly and heavenly rewards according to 1 Corinthians 9:25? Which would you rather have and why?

Third, *our earthly pursuits are temporal, but God's work is eternal.*

Are you currently engaged in ministry? What kind?

What does Hebrews 6:10 say about how God views your ministry?

Albert Camus, the French novelist, understood the ephemeral nature of fame: "At the age of thirty, almost from one day to another, I knew fame . . . and now I know what it amounts to: very little."[7] Very little indeed if all we seek is the applause of humanity. But if we seek to live *soli Deo gloria*, to the glory of God alone, then the Lord applauds from heaven and will not forget to reward us in that glorious day when His fame will fill our eternal home.

LESSON NINE

THE END OF THE AGE

Daniel 12:5–13

THE HEART OF THE MATTER

Human beings are the most unique and frustrated creatures God ever made. Created in God's image (Genesis 1:26), we have the ability to reason, yet we will never be able to completely comprehend the mind of God (Isaiah 55:8–9). This inability often leads to frustration and foolish notions, such as our culture's belief that human reason will someday master divine mysteries.

Daniel, however, even with all of his insight and wisdom, didn't step on the hamster's wheel of the eventual domination of human reason. Instead, in humble dependence, he believed and trusted God to reveal the truth about the last days at the appropriate time—whether or not he could understand it.

DISCOVERING THE WAY

Of all the foolish things men and women have ever believed, none is more foolish than the original lie that we don't need God—that we can figure out the mysteries of the universe on our own. Noted physicist Stephen Hawking illustrated this position eloquently when he wrote, "If we find the answer to [why it is that we and the universe exist], it would be the ultimate triumph of human reason—for then we would know the mind of God."[1]

But if human reason could *triumph* by knowing the mind of God, then what need would we have for God? The obvious answer is none, for we could, in effect, make ourselves gods. Daniel, who came into contact with greater mysteries than Hawking has ever encountered, was not so rigid and arrogant. Daniel understood that there were mysteries beyond his understanding, and he accepted them in faith, trusting in God's perfect wisdom.

Read Daniel 12:8. As we come to the conclusion of our study, do you agree with Daniel that you've read "but could not understand" all that you've studied? Explain.

____

____

Can you accept the fact that you may never fully comprehend some of the mysteries in God's Word? Why, or why not?

____

____

Does this issue affect your relationship with God? In what ways?

____

____

REVIEWING WHERE WE'VE BEEN AND WHERE WE ARE

We have traveled with Daniel through many adventures, but before we come to the final one, let's survey the ground we've covered and reorient ourselves.

You'll recall that the book of Daniel easily divides into two sections. Chapters 1–6 are narrative in nature, telling the story of Daniel and his faithfulness to God while living in the pagan society of Babylon. (You studied these chapters in the *Daniel, Volume 1: God's Man for the Moment Bible Companion.*) Chapters 7–12 are prophetic, filled with Daniel's visions of future events as illustrated by beasts and explained by angels.

Chapter 10, you'll remember, begins with Daniel praying and fasting for three weeks out of his concern for Israel. While standing on the banks of the Tigris River, he saw an angel, most likely Gabriel, who told him of great and terrible wars to come (see Daniel 11). Though many of the wars will be fought in and over the land of Israel, leading to the death of many Jews, the nation ultimately will be protected by the archangel Michael, providing time for some to come to faith in the Messiah (see 12:1–3).

ADDITIONAL EXPLANATION

Read Daniel 12:5–7.

As soon as Gabriel finished speaking (Daniel 12:4), Daniel suddenly saw two additional angels standing on opposite banks of the Tigris (12:5). One asked a question of "the man dressed in linen" (12:6).

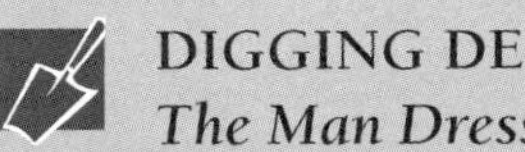

DIGGING DEEPER
The Man Dressed in Linen

Christ made His first entrance dressed in human flesh at Bethlehem, but as the eternal God He sometimes broke into history in human form at other times. Theologians call these events "theophanies" or "preincarnate appearances," meaning that Christ appeared on earth at times before taking on human flesh. For example, Christ ate with Abraham before the destruction of Sodom and Gomorrah (Genesis 18), wrestled with Jacob (Genesis 32:24–30), and presented Himself to Joshua as captain of the Lord's army (Joshua 5:13–15).[2]

Because Daniel's description of the "man dressed in linen" in Daniel 10:5–6 and 12:6–7 is somewhat similar to John's vision of the resurrected Christ in Revelation 1:13–16, some biblical scholars believe that Daniel's "man in linen" is the preincarnate Christ. However, according to respected commentator

Continued on next page

Continued from previous page

J. Dwight Pentecost and others, this explanation is not likely because of "the improbability of Christ being hindered by a prince (demon) of Persia (Daniel 10:13) and needing the help of the angel Michael."[3] Therefore, the man in linen is probably the angel Gabriel, who had previously appeared to Daniel in his visions (see Daniel 7:15–27; 8:15–26; 9:21–27).

"How long will it be until the end of these wonders?" asked one of the other angels standing on the banks of the river (Daniel 12:6). Gabriel, hovering above the river, lifted his hands to heaven and declared that the duration of the great tribulation would be a "time, times, and half a time" (12:7). This time has been fixed by the everlasting God and confirmed in the Scripture.[4]

Read each of the following verses. Noting who wrote or spoke the words, paraphrase that person's request in your own words.

Psalm 79:1–6

____

____

____

Psalm 90:7–9, 13

____

____

____

Jeremiah 12:1–4

___

___

___

Habakkuk 1:1–3

___

___

___

What is the overall theme of these verses?

___

___

___

___

 **Read Daniel 12:8–9.**

The angel's question about the suffering of Israel, "How long?" has echoed throughout the ages in the hearts of Israel's people. Daniel was no exception. In a refreshingly humble admission of the limits of human reason, Daniel confessed: "I heard [all that Gabriel had said] but could not understand" (Daniel 12:8). So he respectfully asked Gabriel what would happen to Israel at the end of the three and a half years (12:8).

What Daniel heard next was not a direct answer to his question. Gabriel told him not to worry about the details of Israel's future but to get back to the business of administering the government—"Go on about your business, Daniel" (12:9 MSG). The visions Daniel saw would be kept safe and secure until the end times.

When studying prophecy, it's easy to get caught up in trying to parse every nuance of a saying, to apply significance to every number, or to determine the exact meaning of unusual descriptions. We can become myopic and miss other truths the Lord is trying to teach us about our lives—always looking to the sky for the Lord's appearing and neglecting the things of the earth. The Thessalonians fell into this trap, and Paul had to correct them. Read 2 Thessalonians 3:7–13. What were they doing and not doing?

____

____

____

____

What did Paul encourage them to do instead?

____

____

____

____

Read Daniel 12:10–13.

Gabriel did allow Daniel to see a glimmer of what will happen to some Jews at the end of the three and a half years. As a result of the persecution in the tribulation, many will come to faith in Jesus Christ as the Messiah, resulting in their spiritual purging, purification, and refinement. But others will continue in their wickedness (Daniel 12:10). Their twisted and distorted minds will keep them bound in their wicked worship of the Antichrist.

Once more returning to the length of the great tribulation, Gabriel provided a few more bits of information, perhaps to remind Daniel that God's plan is specific and will be fulfilled to the smallest detail. We've already seen that the great tribulation will consist of the last three and a half years (or 1,260 days) of the seven-year tribulation period. But Gabriel now told Daniel that from the time the Antichrist abolishes the daily sacrifice and sets up his detestable idol in the temple to the end will constitute "1,290 days" (Daniel 12:11).

What accounts for these thirty additional days? We know that at the end of the great tribulation, when Christ returns to earth, He will first judge Israel (Ezekiel 20:33–38) and the Gentile nations (Matthew 25:31–46). This judgment will include all those who survived the tribulation, winnowing out those who worshiped the Antichrist from those who came to faith in Christ. It is possible that this process will take place during these thirty days.[5]

With the judgment complete, the followers of Christ who survived the tribulation period and the thirty days of judgment will enter into His glorious kingdom (Daniel 12:12). But Gabriel did not end here, with all of the raptured, resurrected, and tribulation saints rejoicing at the commencement of Christ's millennial kingdom. He had a couple more things to say to Daniel. He said those who endure "to the 1,335 days" are blessed. What will take place during these additional forty-five days beyond the 1,290 mentioned in verse 11? This is a mystery, but it seems plausible that this time may include setting up the administrative structure for Christ's millennial kingdom.[6]

We don't know the exact purpose of the thirty- and forty-five-day periods, nor did Daniel. Gabriel concluded by encouraging Daniel with the knowledge that he had work to do for the time being and that at the appointed time God would lay him to rest. Then, when the time was right, Daniel would be resurrected and receive the rewards allotted to him (12:13).[7]

STARTING YOUR JOURNEY

What a wonderful way to end—with resurrection and reward! And as we think about the book of Daniel as a whole, we can see three great truths that will point us to God as we try to make sense of all we have learned and experienced in this study.

First, *the more time we spend with God, the more teachable we become.*

How would you classify the consistency of your time with God?

Nonexistent	
Poor	
Fair	
Good	
Excellent	

How do you feel about the amount of time you spend with God? Do you think you need to make some changes? What are they?

____

____

____

____

____

How teachable are you?

	Rate Yourself	Have Someone Else Rate You
Not Very		
Somewhat		
Very		

Do you think your time with God affects your level of teachability? How might your level of teachability affect your relationship with God?

Second, *the more questions we ask, the more dependent we become.*

Now that you've studied the book of Daniel, what questions do you still have about the future?

Where do you think the answers to these questions can be found?

Pause here and write a prayer asking God to help you find answers to these questions.

Dear God,

____

____

____

____

____

____

Third, *the more truth we discover, the more profound it becomes.*

Think back over your study of Daniel, and list some of the truths you've discovered in this book.

____

____

____

____

____

Of these truths, which three do you consider the most profound?

1. ____

2. ____

3. ____

What will you do to apply these three truths in your everyday life? Be specific.

____

____

____

____

The wily sage of colonial America, Benjamin Franklin, wrote that "Experience keeps a dear School, but Fools will learn in no other, and scarce in that."[8] For all of our intelligence, of our study of the heavens and the depths of the sea, of our hope for enlightenment and understanding, the truth is, our finite minds will never comprehend infinity or eternity. No one captured this truth better than French mathematician Blaise Pascal:

> Reason's last step is the recognition that there are an infinite number of things which are beyond it. It is merely feeble if it does not go as far as to realize that.
>
> If natural things are beyond it, what are we to say about supernatural things?[9]

Daniel, and we, may not understand every detail written in his book, but we can understand, just as he did, that possessing a teachable spirit, learning to lean on our sovereign God alone, and realizing that God's wisdom is far greater than our understanding combine to create a sure path away from folly and toward truth. And that's a reasonable conclusion if there ever was one.

As a fun review of the book of Daniel, complete this crossword puzzle. If you get stuck, look up the answer key (page 128).

Across

2. The foolish king who witnessed the handwriting on the wall in Daniel 5

5. The kingdom represented by the chest and arms of silver in Daniel 2:31–49

9. The kings of the South in Daniel 11

13. The last three and a half years of the "time of distress" (two words)

14. The Son of Man (Jesus _____)

16. The Ancient of Days

17. The kingdom represented by the legs of iron in Daniel 2:31–49

18. The ruler known as "the Mede" (Daniel 5:31; 11:1)

20. Shadrach, Meshach, and Abed-nego didn't find this too hot (two words)

21. The first name of the man represented by the large horn in Daniel 8:21

Down

1. The kingdom represented by the thighs of bronze in Daniel 2:31–49

2. The kingdom represented by the head of gold in Daniel 2:38

3. Daniel's punishment for prayer in Daniel 6:13–16 (two words)

4. The kings of the North in Daniel 11

6. God's man in Babylon

7. How the Bible describes 490 years in Daniel 9:24 (two words)

8. The next event on God's prophetic calendar

10. God's "Beautiful Land" (Daniel 8:9; 11:16)

11. The great king who went insane in Daniel 4

12. The world dictator represented by the fourth beast in Daniel 7:8

13. The angel who explained prophecy in Daniel 8:16

15. The person represented by the little horn in Daniel 8:9

19. The angelic protector of Israel (Daniel 12:1)

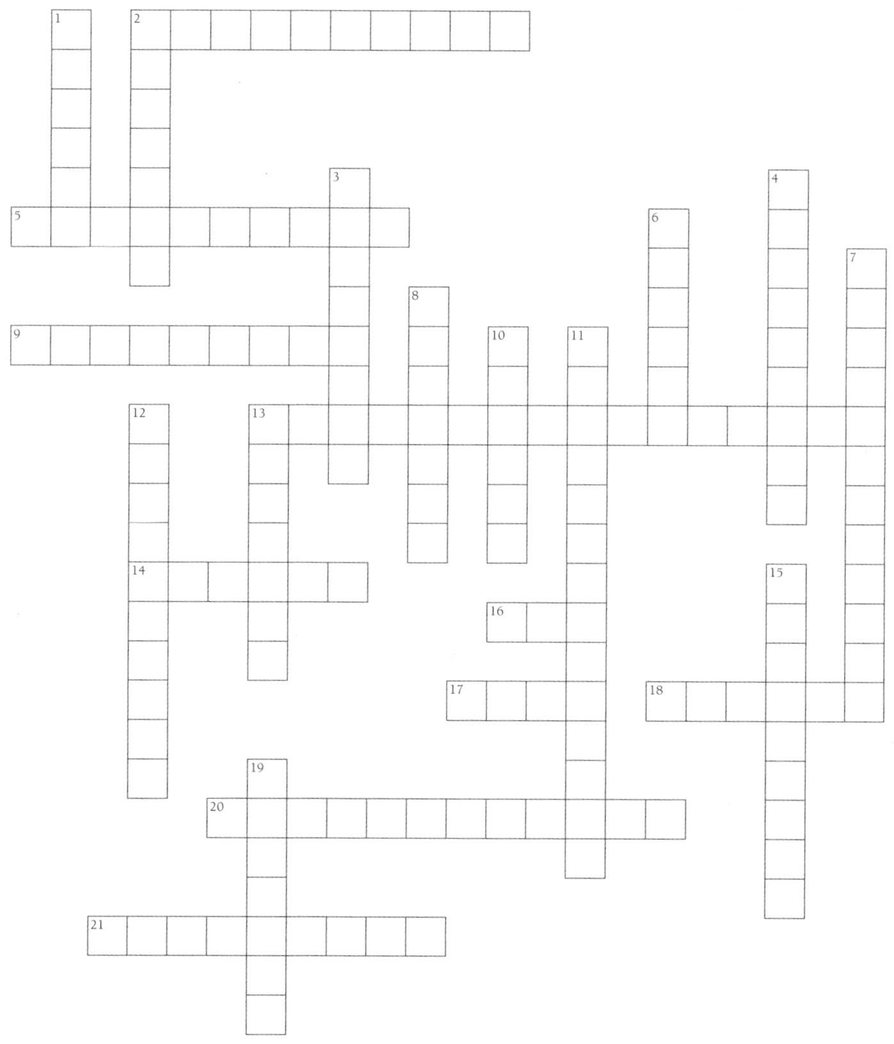
1
2
3
4
5
6
7
8
9
10
11
12
13
14
15
16
17
18
19
20
21

HOW TO BEGIN A RELATIONSHIP WITH GOD

With God, promises made are promises kept. His meticulous prophecies concerning Babylon, Persia, Greece, Egypt, Syria, and Antiochus Epiphanes were fulfilled down to the smallest detail. This history should remind us that what God has promised for the future will be kept according to His calendar. So the question that demands an answer is not, will God keep His promises about the end of time, but, will we be ready when that time comes?

The answer to that question is found in another promise, the greatest promise God ever made—the incarnation, death, and resurrection of the Messiah (Daniel 9:26). The Messiah is none other than Jesus Christ, who kept God's promise, offering salvation and eternal life to all who desire a relationship with Him. If you're interested in such a relationship, the Bible marks the path to God with four essential truths. Let's look at each marker in detail.

OUR SPIRITUAL CONDITION: TOTALLY DEPRAVED

The first truth is rather personal. One look in the mirror of Scripture, and our human condition becomes painfully clear:

> There is none righteous, not even one;
> There is none who understands,
> There is none who seeks for God;
> All have turned aside, together they have become
> useless;
> There is none who does good,
> There is not even one. (Romans 3:10–12)

We are all sinners through and through—totally depraved. Now, that doesn't mean we've committed every atrocity known to humankind. We're not as *bad* as we can be, just as *bad off* as we can be. Sin colors all our thoughts, motives, words, and actions.

You still don't believe it? Look around. Everything around us bears the smudge marks of our sinful nature. In spite of our best efforts to create a perfect world, crime statistics continue to soar, divorce rates keep climbing, and families keep crumbling.

Something has gone terribly wrong in our society and in ourselves—something deadly. Contrary to how the world would repackage it, "me-first" living doesn't equal rugged individuality and freedom; it equals death. As Paul said in his letter to the Romans, "The wages of sin is death" (Romans 6:23)—our spiritual and physical death that comes from God's righteous judgment of our sin, along with all of the emotional and practical effects of this separation that we experience on a daily basis. This brings us to the second marker: God's character.

GOD'S CHARACTER: INFINITELY HOLY

How can God judge each of us for a sinful state we were born into? Our total depravity is only half the answer. The other half is God's infinite holiness.

The fact that we know things are not as they should be points us to a standard of goodness beyond ourselves. Our sense of injustice in life on this side of eternity implies a perfect standard of justice beyond our reality. That standard and source is God Himself. And God's standard of holiness contrasts starkly with our sinful condition.

Scripture says that "God is Light, and in Him there is no darkness at all" (1 John 1:5). God is absolutely holy—which creates a problem for us. If He is so pure, how can we who are so impure relate to Him?

Perhaps we could try being better people, try to tilt the balance in favor of our good deeds, or seek out methods for self-improvement. Throughout history, people have attempted to live up to God's standard by keeping the Ten Commandments or living by their own code of ethics. Unfortunately, no one can come close to satisfying the demands of God's law. Romans 3:20 says, "By the works of the Law no flesh will be justified in His sight; for through the Law comes the knowledge of sin."

OUR NEED: A SUBSTITUTE

So here we are, sinners by nature and sinners by choice, trying to pull ourselves up by our own bootstraps to attain a relationship with our holy Creator. But every time we try, we fall flat on our faces. We can't live a good enough life to make up for our sin, because God's standard isn't "good enough"—it's *perfection*. And we can't make amends for the offense our sin has created without dying for it.

Who can get us out of this mess?

If someone could live perfectly, honoring God's law, and would bear sin's death penalty for us—in our place—then we would be saved from our predicament. But is there such a person? Thankfully, yes!

Meet your substitute—*Jesus Christ*. He is the One who took death's place for you!

> [God] made [Jesus Christ] who knew no sin to be sin on our behalf, so that we might become the righteousness of God in Him. (2 Corinthians 5:21)

GOD'S PROVISION: A SAVIOR

God rescued us by sending His Son, Jesus, to die on the cross for our sins (1 John 4:9–10). Jesus was fully human and fully divine (John 1:1, 18), a truth that ensures His understanding of our weaknesses, His power to forgive, and His ability to bridge the gap between God and us (Romans 5:6–11). In short, we are "justified as a gift by His grace through the redemption which is in Christ Jesus" (3:24). Two words in this verse bear further explanation: *justified* and *redemption*.

Justification is God's act of mercy, in which He declares believing sinners righteous, while they are still in their sinning state. Justification doesn't mean that God *makes* us righteous, so that we never sin again, rather that He *declares* us righteous—much like a judge pardons a guilty criminal. Because Jesus took our sin upon Himself and suffered our judgment on the cross, God forgives our debt and proclaims us PARDONED.

Redemption is Christ's act of paying the price to release us from sin's bondage. God sent His Son to bear His wrath for all of our sins—past, present, and future (Romans 3:24–26; 2 Corinthians 5:21). In humble obedience, Christ willingly endured the shame of the cross for your sake (Mark 10:45; Romans 5:6–8; Philippians 2:8). Christ's death satisfied God's righteous demands. He no longer holds your sins against you, because His own Son paid the penalty for them. You are freed from the slave market of death, never to be a slave again!

PLACING YOUR FAITH IN CHRIST

These four truths describe how God has provided a way to Himself through Jesus Christ. Because the price has been paid in full by God, we must respond to His free gift of eternal life in total faith and confidence in Him to save us. We must step forward into the relationship with God that He has prepared for us—not by doing good works or by being a good person but by coming to Him just as we are and accepting His justification and redemption by faith.

> For by grace you have been saved through faith; and that not of yourselves, it is the gift of God; not as a result of works, so that no one may boast. (Ephesians 2:8–9)

We accept God's gift of salvation simply by placing our faith in Christ alone for the forgiveness of our sins. Would you like to enter a relationship with your Creator by trusting in Christ as your Savior? If so, here's a simple prayer you can use to express your faith:

> *Dear God,*
>
> *I know that my sin has put a barrier between You and me. Thank You for sending Your Son, Jesus, to die in my place. I trust in Jesus alone to forgive my sins, and I accept His gift of eternal life. I ask Jesus to be my personal Savior and the Lord of my life. Thank You. In Jesus's name, amen.*

If you've prayed this prayer or one like it and you wish to find out more about knowing God and His plan for you in the Bible, contact us at Insight for Living. You can speak to one of our pastors on staff by using the information below:

Insight for Living
Pastoral Ministries Department
Post Office Box 269000
Plano, Texas 75026-9000
USA
972-473-5097 (Monday through Friday
8:00 a.m.–5:00 p.m. Central time)
www.insight.org/contactapastor

WE ARE HERE FOR YOU

If you desire to find out more about knowing God and His plan for you in the Bible, contact us. Insight for Living provides staff pastors who are available for free written correspondence or phone consultation. These seminary-trained and seasoned counselors have years of experience and are well-qualified guides for your spiritual journey.

Please feel welcome to contact your regional Pastoral Ministries department by using the information below:

United States

Insight for Living
Pastoral Ministries Department
Post Office Box 269000
Plano, Texas 75026-9000
972-473-5097, Monday through Friday,
8:00 a.m.–5:00 p.m. Central time
www.insight.org/contactapastor

Canada

Insight for Living Canada
Pastoral Ministries Department
Post Office Box 2510
Vancouver, BC V6B 3W7
CANADA
1-604-870-8742

Australia, New Zealand, and South Pacific

Insight for Living Australia
Pastoral Care
Post Office Box 1011
Bayswater, VIC 3153
AUSTRALIA
1 300 467 444

United Kingdom and Europe

Insight for Living United Kingdom
Pastoral Care
Post Office Box 348
Leatherhead
KT22 2DS
UNITED KINGDOM
0800 9159364
+44 (0) 1372 370055
pastoralcare@insightforliving.org.uk

ENDNOTES

Unless otherwise noted below, all material in this Bible Companion is adapted from the *Daniel: God's Plan for the Future* sermon series by Charles R. Swindoll and was supplemented by the Creative Ministries department of Insight for Living.

A LETTER FROM CHUCK

1. Winston S. Churchill, "The First Month of War" (October 1, 1939), quoted in *Churchill Speaks, 1897–1963: Collected Speeches in Peace & War*, ed. Robert Rhodes James (New York: Barnes and Noble Books, 1998), 694.

LESSON ONE

1. Winston S. Churchill, comments at Cairo Press Conference (February 1, 1943), in Dominique Enright, *The Wicked Wit of Winston Churchill* (London: Michael O'Mara Books, 2001), 18.
2. Warren W. Wiersbe, "Daniel," in *The Wiersbe Bible Commentary: The Complete Old Testament in One Volume* (Colorado Springs: David C. Cook, 2007), 1369.
3. See J. Dwight Pentecost, "Daniel," in *The Bible Knowledge Commentary: Old Testament*, ed. John F. Walvoord and Roy B. Zuck (Wheaton, Ill.: Victor Books, 1986), 1349. Also see Wiersbe, "Daniel," 1368.
4. Pentecost believed that Daniel was about 16 years old when he was taken captive in 605 BC and calculated his age from there. See Pentecost, "Daniel," 1349.
5. The Aramaic word *ruach* can also be translated as "wind" or "spirit." This word is often used in the Bible to describe the Holy Spirit and

sometimes used to describe angels. See Francis Brown, S. R. Driver, and Charles A. Briggs, *The Brown-Driver-Briggs Hebrew and English Lexicon* (Peabody, Mass.: Hendrickson, 2006), 1112. This word is used elsewhere in Scripture in reference to God's providential working in the affairs of men (Jeremiah 23:19; 49:36; Zechariah 6:1–6; 7:14; Revelation 7:1–3). Theologian John F. Walvoord affirms that "the symbolism of winds striving with the sea may represent God's power as He deals with sinful man to attain divine ends." John F. Walvoord, "End Times: Understanding Today's World Events in Biblical Prophecy," in *Understanding Christian Theology*, ed. Charles R. Swindoll and Roy B. Zuck (Nashville: Thomas Nelson, 2003), 1304.

6. The "Great Sea" is a common designation for the Mediterranean Sea in the Bible (Numbers 34:6–7; Joshua 1:4; 9:1; 15:12, 47; 23:4; Ezekiel 47:10, 15, 20; 48:28). Though Daniel 7:3 says that the four beasts came "up from the sea," the interpretation given by the angel in Daniel 7:17 says that these beasts arose "from the earth." Therefore, it seems better to view the sea as a symbol of the Gentile nations (see Isaiah 17:12–13; Revelation 17:15).

7. Bible scholars have come up with three common interpretations of the three ribs in Daniel 7:5. First, they may represent the three dominant kingdoms that preceded the Medo-Persian Empire: Egypt, Assyria, and Babylon. Second, they could represent the three kingdoms conquered by the Medes and Persians: Babylon, Lydia, and Egypt. Third, they might represent three provinces of the Medes and Persians: Babylonia, Persia, and Media. See Pentecost, "Daniel," 1350; John F. Walvoord, *The Prophecy Knowledge Handbook* (Wheaton, Ill.: SP Publications, 1990), 231.

8. Even though Daniel 7:16 doesn't explicitly mention the angel Gabriel by name, Gabriel was sent by God to help Daniel interpret a later vision (Daniel 8:15–16). Gabriel also appeared to Daniel during his prayer in 9:21. It is a likely assumption that Gabriel was also the interpreter of Daniel 7:15–27.

9. Some scholars hold that a form of Roman rule, as represented by the ten horns, remained after the collapse of the Roman Empire in the

fifth century AD and continues to this day (see Pentecost, "Daniel," 1354). Others interpret the ten horns as a future revived or restored Roman Empire (Revelation 13:1; 17:12); see Donald K. Campbell, *Daniel: God's Man in a Secular Society* (Grand Rapids: Discovery House, 1988), 113.

10. For more information on the millennial kingdom, see Walvoord, "End Times," 1350–62.

LESSON TWO

1. Fyodor Dostoevsky, *The Brothers Karamazov*, trans. Richard Pevear and Larissa Volokhonsky (New York: Knopf, 1992), 257.

2. For more information on the rapture, see Insight for Living, *Daniel, Volume 1: God's Man for the Moment Bible Companion* (Plano, Tex.: IFL Publishing House, 2008), 8–9. According to the *pretribulational* view to which conservative Bible teachers such as Chuck Swindoll, John F. Walvoord, and Dwight Pentecost ascribe, the rapture will occur before the seven year period known as the tribulation. Their reasoning is as follows: First, in 1 Thessalonians 4:13–18, Paul implied that the rapture is the next event in God's prophetic plan. Second, the sudden and unexpected nature of Christ's second advent or second coming, which will happen at the end of the tribulation, indicates that the rapture must come first (Luke 12:40). Finally, they hold to Christ's promise to keep the church "from the hour of testing" (Revelation 3:10). Other views on the rapture include the *midtribulational* position, which says that the church will suffer through the first three and a half years of the tribulation before being removed, and the *posttribulational* view that believes the church will endure the complete seven years. This view, in particular, blurs the distinction between the rapture and the second advent. See John F. Walvoord, "End Times: Understanding Today's World Events in Biblical Prophecy," in *Understanding Christian Theology*, ed. Charles R. Swindoll and Roy B. Zuck (Nashville: Thomas Nelson, 2003), 1264–68, for a thorough treatment of the various views of the rapture.

3. Walter Bauer and others, *A Greek-English Lexicon of the New Testament and other Early Christian Literature*, 3d ed., rev. and ed. Frederick William Danker (Chicago: University of Chicago, 2000), 87.

4. Bauer and others, *A Greek-English Lexicon of the New Testament and other Early Christian Literature*, 87.

5. These saints are sometimes called tribulation saints, because they will come to faith in Christ after the rapture, during the seven years of tribulation.

6. Leon Morris, *The First and Second Epistles to the Thessalonians*, rev. ed., The New International Commentary on the New Testament (Grand Rapids: Eerdmans, 1991), 220.

7. See Isaiah 27:1; Revelation 12:3–4, 7–9, 13–17; 20:1–3, 7–10 for more information about the dragon, Satan.

8. The leopard represented Greece, the bear was Medo-Persia, and the lion was Babylon (see Daniel 7:2–8).

9. The interpretation of the Beast's "fatal wound" is complicated. Some have interpreted the beast's "fatal wound" as a political blow that he survives. Most conservative commentators agree that Satan does not have the power to raise anyone from the dead—only the Creator has the authority and ability to give life. Thus they believe that the Antichrist will survive some sort of devastating physical wound. For further discussion of this issue, see John F. Walvoord, *The Prophecy Knowledge Handbook* (Wheaton, Ill.: SP Publications, 1990), 582–83.

10. Many through the ages have attempted to identify the Antichrist by assigning numerical values to Hebrew, Greek, and Latin letters and calculating the "number" of certain names. The fact of the matter is, the Antichrist's identity will not be clear until after the rapture when he is revealed (2 Thessalonians 2:3).

11. With the introduction of the False Prophet, the "unholy trinity" is complete and in mocking opposition to the Holy Trinity. The dragon, Satan, presumes the role of the Father, God. The Antichrist mimics the role of the Son, Jesus Christ. And the False Prophet assumes the

role of the Holy Spirit. Unlike the Holy Spirit, who woos Christians to worship the Father and the Son, the False Prophet will encourage people to worship the Antichrist.

LESSON THREE

1. Charles W. Colson, "The Enduring Revolution," in *Chuck Colson Speaks: Twelve Key Messages from Today's Leading Defender of the Christian Faith* (Uhrichsville, Ohio: Promise, 2000), 18.

2. This vision occurred in 550 BC when Daniel was approximately 71 years old. See lesson 1, "A Prophetic Collage," page 3, for a chronology of Belshazzar's reign.

3. Elam came under Babylonian control during the reign of Nebuchadnezzar, but at the time it was not a significant city. The Ulai Canal may have carried water into the city. See John J. Collins, *Daniel: A Commentary on the Book of Daniel*, Hermeneia—A Critical and Historical Commentary on the Bible (Minneapolis: Augsburg Fortress, 1993), 329. Susa itself would later become, in the words of the ancient Jewish historian Josephus, "the metropolis of Persia." Flavius Josephus, *The Antiquities of the Jews*, 10.11.7, in *Josephus: Complete Works*, trans. William Whiston (Grand Rapids: Kregel, 1976), 227.

4. The "rather small horn" in Daniel 8 is *not* the same as the "little horn" in Daniel 7. The "little horn" will arise out of the "fourth empire [Roman] and in its final stage which, properly interpreted, still refers to the future." The "small horn" came out of the "third kingdom [Greece], the goat, and refers to prophecy that has already been fulfilled." John F. Walvoord, *The Prophecy Knowledge Handbook* (Wheaton, Ill.: SP Publications, 1990), 238.

5. Though his presence can be inferred at other times (see lesson 1, "A Prophetic Collage," note 8), this is the first time Gabriel is mentioned in the Scriptures. There are only four references to him by name: as a messenger and interpreter in Daniel 8:16 and Daniel 9:21; in Luke 1:19 giving a message to Zacharias about the birth of

John the Baptist; and in Luke 1:26 announcing to Mary the conception of Jesus.

6. Gabriel's use of the term "son of man" was simply meant to identify Daniel as being from the race of men and should be distinguished from Daniel's description of the Messiah in Daniel 7:13.

7. Philip II of Macedonia was the first to unite the once fiercely independent Greek city-states into a kingdom. But his son, Alexander, was considered to be Greece's first actual king.

8. Walvoord, *The Prophecy Knowledge Handbook*, 231.

9. The Greek word *epiphanes* means "splendid" or "glorious." Walter Bauer and others, *A Greek-English Lexicon of the New Testament and other Early Christian Literature*, 3d ed., rev. and ed. Frederick William Danker (Chicago: University of Chicago, 2000), 386. Many Jews "called him Epimanes, the 'madman' . . . a play on words on the title which he himself affected later in his reign . . . Epiphanes (or more fully *Theos Epiphanes*, 'God Manifest')." F. F. Bruce, *Israel and the Nations* (Grand Rapids: Eerdmans, 1983), 135.

10. Bruce, *Israel and the Nations*, 138–42.

11. Antiochus's act became known as the "abomination of desolation" in Jewish history; see also Daniel 9:27; 11:31; 12:11; Matthew 24:15.

12. See Josephus, *The Antiquities of the Jews*, 12.5.4, 257; Bruce, *Israel and the Nations*, 146; and J. Dwight Pentecost, "Daniel," in *The Bible Knowledge Commentary: Old Testament*, ed. John F. Walvoord and Roy B. Zuck (Wheaton, Ill: Victor Books, 1986), 1358.

13. Bruce, *Israel and the Nations*, 147–53, for a complete treatment of the Jewish resistance against Antiochus and the final restoration of the temple, later celebrated in the Jewish calendar as Hanukkah.

14. Antiochus died in 164 BC, possibly as the result of illness or accident. Various ancient "accounts agree in stating that the tyrant met his end by a nonhuman agency." See Kenneth L. Barker and

John R. Kohlenberger, eds., *The Expositor's Bible Commentary: Old Testament*, abridged ed. (Grand Rapids: Zondervan, 1994), 1385–86.

15. Thucydides, *History of the Peloponnesian War*, in *The Landmark Thucydides: A Comprehensive Guide to The Peloponnesian War*, 1.22.4, trans. Richard Crawley, ed. Robert B. Strassler (New York: Touchstone Books, 1998), 16.

LESSON FOUR

1. Samuel Davies, "On the Defeat of General Braddock, Going to Fort Duquesne," in *Sermons by the Rev. Samuel Davies*, vol. III (Philadelphia: Presbyterian Board of Publication, 1864), 311.

2. For more information regarding the identity of Darius the Mede, see Insight for Living, *Daniel, Volume 1: God's Man for the Moment Bible Companion* (Plano, Tex.: IFL Publishing House, 2008), 78–79.

3. The seventy-year time period was directly connected to God's command to observe a "Sabbath year" every seven years to allow the land to rest (Leviticus 25:2–7). The Lord promised that if the people disobeyed, He would remove them from the land for a time (Leviticus 26:34–35, 43). And when the Jews deprived the land of seventy Sabbaths over a 490-year span, God kept His Word, resulting in their seventy-year captivity (2 Chronicles 36:20–21).

4. Francis Brown, S. R. Driver, and Charles A. Briggs, *The Brown-Driver-Briggs Hebrew and English Lexicon* (Peabody, Mass.: Hendrickson, 2006), 306.

5. Brown, Driver, and Briggs, *The Brown-Driver-Briggs Hebrew and English Lexicon*, 730.

6. Brown, Driver, and Briggs, *The Brown-Driver-Briggs Hebrew and English Lexicon*, 957.

7. Brown, Driver, and Briggs, *The Brown-Driver-Briggs Hebrew and English Lexicon*, 597.

8. Brown, Driver, and Briggs, *The Brown-Driver-Briggs Hebrew and English Lexicon*, 693.

9. Thomas Paine, "The American Crisis, Number I," in *Thomas Paine: Collected Writings* (New York: The Library of America, 1995), 91.

10. Benjamin Franklin, quoted in Carl Van Doren, *Benjamin Franklin* (New York: Viking, 1938), 747–48.

LESSON FIVE

1. Lewis Carroll, *Through the Looking-Glass and What Alice Found There*, in *The Annotated Alice: The Definitive Edition* (New York: Norton, 2000), 253.

2. 7 x 7 = 49; 62 x 7 = 434; 49 + 434 = 483=x.
   3.5 x 2 = 7 + 483 = 490=y.

3. For *sakal*, see Francis Brown, S. R. Driver, and Charles A. Briggs, *The Brown-Driver-Briggs Hebrew and English Lexicon* (Peabody, Mass.: Hendrickson, 2006), 968. For *binah*, see Brown, Driver, and Briggs, *The Brown-Driver-Briggs Hebrew and English Lexicon*, 108.

4. Donald K. Campbell, *Daniel: God's Man in a Secular Society* (Grand Rapids: Discovery House, 1988), 148.

5. The Hebrew word *shabua* refers to a "period of seven" days or years. Brown, Driver, and Briggs, *The Brown-Driver-Briggs Hebrew and English Lexicon*, 988.

6. Daniel used the same Hebrew word, *shabua*, in Daniel 10:2 but added the word for "day," *yom*, literally rendering this verse as "three days of seven" (or twenty-one days). Daniel's use of *yom* in Daniel 10:2 distinguishes the calculation from Daniel 9:24—one speaks of days and the other speaks of years.

7. Each "week" represents seven years. So "seven weeks" is 7 x 7 or forty-nine years; "sixty-two weeks" is 62 x 7 or 434 years; and "one

week" is 1 x 7 or seven years. Added together the total number of "weeks" equals 490 years.

8. See J. Dwight Pentecost, "Daniel," in *The Bible Knowledge Commentary: Old Testament*, ed. John F. Walvoord and Roy B. Zuck (Wheaton, Ill.: Victor Books, 1986), 1361–62; and Campbell, *Daniel*, 141.

9. Four decrees were issued by Persian kings concerning Israel, the rebuilding of the temple, and Jerusalem. The first decree was issued by Cyrus the Great in 538 BC, allowing the Jews to rebuild the temple and spurring a large group to return to the Promised Land (2 Chronicles 36:22–23; Ezra 1:1–4; 5:13). The second decree was a reaffirmation and confirmation of Cyrus's decree issued by Darius I in 520 BC (Ezra 6:1, 6–12). The third decree, issued by Artaxerxes Longimanus in 457 BC, provided financial assistance for sacrifices in the temple (Ezra 7:11–26). The fourth decree, also issued by Artaxerxes Longimanus, came in 444 BC, and it specifically told the Jews to rebuild Jerusalem. See John F. Walvoord, "End Times: Understanding Today's World Events in Biblical Prophecy," in *Understanding Christian Theology*, ed. Charles R. Swindoll and Roy B. Zuck (Nashville: Thomas Nelson, 2003), 1311–12.

10. Remember, Daniel's prayer and Gabriel's visit occurred in the first year of Darius the Mede's reign (Daniel 9:1), or 538 BC. See Walvoord, "End Times," 1312; and Harold W. Hoehner, *Chronological Aspects of the Life of Christ* (Grand Rapids: Academie Books, 1977), 138, for the exact dating of Artaxerxes's decree.

11. Traditionally this is known as the triumphal entry (Matthew 21:1–11; Mark 11:1–10; Luke 19:29–38). Four days later, on April 3, AD 33, Christ was crucified. See Walvoord, "End Times," 1312; and Hoehner, *Chronological Aspects of the Life of Christ*, 138–39, for exact dating of Christ's entrance into Jerusalem and death.

12. The comparison chart between the Jewish and Gregorian calendars is from Pentecost, "Daniel," 1363. This chart is copyright 1985 by Cook Communication Ministries. *The Bible Knowledge Commentary: Old Testament*, ed. John F. Walvoord and Roy B. Zuck. Used with

permission. May not be further reproduced. All rights reserved. The Jewish calendar is based on the lunar cycle or thirty days a month. The Gregorian (modern) calendar is based on the solar cycle which requires adjustments. The chart is converted into days to show the precision of the prophecy.

13. Only one year expired between 1 BC and AD 1, which accounts for 476 years rather than 477 years.

14. A total of 476 years divided by four (a leap year every four years) equals 119 additional days. However, three days must be subtracted from 119 because centennial years are not leap years, though every 400th year is a leap year.

15. According to modern astronomy, a year equals precisely 365 days, 5 hours, 48 minutes, and 45 seconds. After calculating 365-day years plus leap years, additional days must be added into the equation. See Hoehner, *Chronological Aspects of the Life of Christ*, 135, 138.

16. Jesus predicted this in Matthew 23:38; 24:2; and Luke 21:24. The ancient Jewish historian Josephus gives a very short account of Jerusalem's and the temple's destruction. Flavius Josephus, *The Wars of the Jews*, 7.1.1., in *Josephus: Complete Works*, trans. William Whiston (Grand Rapids: Kregel, 1976), 589.

17. The book of Leviticus, in particular, outlines the various forms and means of the Jewish sacrificial system.

18. See 2 Thessalonians 2:3–4 and Revelation 13:8, 14–15. Christ warned that the Antichrist would bring "the abomination of desolation" to the "holy place" (Matthew 24:15).

LESSON SIX

1. H. L. Mencken, *Minority Report: H. L. Mencken's Notebooks* (New York: Knopf, 1956), 241.

2. Because of the way kings' reigns were dated, these years are a bit difficult to reconcile exactly. For help, see Insight for Living,

Daniel, Volume 1: God's Man for the Moment Bible Companion (Plano, Tex.: IFL Publishing House, 2008), 110, note 3.

3. Ezra 1–6 provides details about this return to Jerusalem, but generally about fifty thousand Jews returned under the leadership of Zerubbabel and laid the foundation of the temple. The temple itself was not completed until 515 BC under the reign of Darius I (Ezra 6:15).

4. Bible scholars have often debated the identity of this "man." It seems best to see him as an angel for several reasons. First, angels acted as messengers or interpreters for Daniel several times already (see Daniel 7:15–27; 8:15–26; 9:21–27). And Daniel 11–12 also recounts Daniel's interaction with an angel. In all of these cases, it is likely that the angel was Gabriel. He is identified by name in 8:16 and 9:21. And notice that in 11:1, the angel mentions that he has been supporting Darius the Mede since the first year of his reign—the same time that Gabriel interpreted the meaning of Daniel's vision of the seventy "sevens" in Daniel 9.

5. We know the "prince of Persia" was a demon because he acted in opposition to God's angel. Also, no mere man could have resisted God's holy messenger. See Donald K. Campbell, *Daniel: God's Man in a Secular Society* (Grand Rapids: Discovery House, 1988), 155. Because of this reference to the prince of Persia and the angel's warning about the coming of the prince of Greece (Daniel 10:20), many scholars have examined the idea that earthly kingdoms might have been assigned demon "princes." Scholar John J. Collins writes that "the notion that different nations were allotted to different gods or heavenly beings was widespread in the ancient world." See John J. Collins, *Daniel: A Commentary on the Book of Daniel*, Hermeneia—A Critical and Historical Commentary on the Bible (Minneapolis: Augsburg Fortress, 1993), 374; and J. Dwight Pentecost, "Daniel," in *The Bible Knowledge Commentary: Old Testament*, ed. John F. Walvoord and Roy B. Zuck (Wheaton, Ill.: Victor Books, 1986), 1366.

6. See Henry W. Holloman, "Sanctification: Rediscovering the Transforming Power of Sanctification," in *Understanding Christian Theology*, ed. Charles R. Swindoll and Roy B. Zuck (Nashville: Thomas Nelson, 2003), 1035–39.

7. This is the first time the Bible mentions Michael by name. In fact, only two angels in the Bible are given proper names—Michael and Gabriel. Michael is called "one of the chief princes" (Daniel 10:13), "the great prince" (Daniel 12:1), or "archangel" (Jude 9). Michael is the commander of the holy angels who will lead them into the heavenly battle against the dragon, Satan, during the last days (Revelation 12:7). The Bible seems to rank angels and demons (see Romans 8:38; Ephesians 1:21; 3:10; 6:12), which may account for why the angelic messenger couldn't overcome the demon until a higher-ranked angel, Michael, arrived. For a comprehensive treatment of angels and demons, see Robert P. Lightner, "Angels, Satan, and Demons: Invisible Beings that Inhabit the Spiritual World," in *Understanding Christian Theology*, ed. Charles R. Swindoll and Roy B. Zuck (Nashville: Thomas Nelson, 2003), 537–640.

8. The "Book of Truth" (Daniel 10:21 NIV) is probably a divine record of human history, written beforehand, that may include the Bible (see Pentecost, "Daniel," 1367). Be careful; don't confuse it with the famed "book of life" (Revelation 20:15; 21:27) that lists the names of Christ's followers.

LESSON SEVEN

1. Harry S. Truman, "Address in San Francisco at the Closing Session of the United Nations Conference" (June 26, 1945), http://trumanlibrary.org/publicpapers/viewpapers.php?pid=73, accessed March 19, 2008.

2. Donald K. Campbell, *Daniel: God's Man in a Secular Society* (Grand Rapids: Discovery House, 1988), 162. The remaining verses provide details of what is to come during the tribulation.

3. Most scholars agree that the four kings were Cambyses (529–523 BC); Pseudo-Smerdis (an imposter who took the throne under false

pretenses and reigned from 522–521 BC); Darius I Hystaspes, also called Darius the Great (522–485 BC; see Ezra 5–6); and Xerxes I (485–464 BC; see Ezra 4:6), who was known as Ahasuerus in the book of Esther. See J. Dwight Pentecost, "Daniel," in *The Bible Knowledge Commentary: Old Testament*, ed. John F. Walvoord and Roy B. Zuck (Wheaton, Ill.: Victor Books, 1986), 1367; and Kenneth L. Barker and John R. Kohlenberger III, eds., *The Expositor's Bible Commentary: Old Testament*, abridged ed. (Grand Rapids: Zondervan, 1994), 1392–93.

4. Xerxes I did marshal an army and navy against Athens, but he was ultimately unsuccessful in capturing the city. His navy was defeated at the battle of Salamis in 480 BC, and his army was decimated at the battle of Plataea in 479 BC. See F. F. Bruce, *Israel and the Nations* (Grand Rapids: Eerdmans, 1963), 120.

5. Campbell, *Daniel*, 164.

6. The historical facts of this period have been gleaned from Campbell, *Daniel*, 165–67; John J. Collins, *Daniel: A Commentary on the Book of Daniel*, Hermeneia—A Critical and Historical Commentary on the Bible (Minneapolis: Augsburg Fortress, 1993), 378–82; Pentecost, "Daniel," 1368–69; and John F. Walvoord, *The Prophecy Knowledge Handbook* (Wheaton, Ill.: SP Publications, 1990), 265–68.

7. His successor, Antiochus I Soter (281–262 BC), is not referred to in the account of Daniel 11.

8. Be careful not to confuse Cleopatra I (Daniel 11:17) with Cleopatra VII. The latter ruled in Egypt from 51–31 BC, and she is best known for her relationships with Julius Caesar and Mark Antony.

9. The historical facts of this period have been gleaned from Campbell, *Daniel*, 167–69; Collins, *Daniel*, 382–86; Pentecost, "Daniel," 1369–70; and Walvoord, *The Prophecy Knowledge Handbook*, 268–71.

10. Antiochus IV Epiphanes appointed Jason (the Greek rendering of Joshua), the brother of Onias, as high priest after Jason promised to

Hellenize, or promote Greek culture and language, in Jerusalem and pay a hefty tribute. See Bruce, *Israel and the Nations*, 135.

11. See Collins, *Daniel*, 383.

12. The "ships of Kittim" (Daniel 11:30) is a reference to the Roman navy that sailed from Cyprus and came to Egypt's defense. Antiochus IV Epiphanes was met on the outskirts of Alexandria by his old Roman friend Lucius Popillius Laenas, who, instead of taking Antiochus's hand in friendship, placed within his hand a decree from the Roman Senate ordering him to leave Egypt. When Antiochus asked for time to consult with his counselors, Laenas drew a circle around Antiochus in the sand and demanded an answer before he stepped out of the circle. Antiochus had no choice but to leave Egypt in disgrace. See Bruce, *Israel and the Nations*, 141–42.

13. The most famous son, Judas Maccabaeus, "the Hammer," cleaned the temple of Antiochus IV Epiphanes's sacrilege and restored the sacred sacrifices, as promised in Daniel 8:14. See Bruce, *Israel and the Nations*, 147–53, for a complete treatment of the Jewish resistance against Antiochus and the restoration of the temple.

14. Most reliable commentators believe that the phrase "He will show no . . . desire of women" (Daniel 11:37) should not be interpreted to mean that the Antichrist will be a homosexual or that he will have complete mastery over sexual desire. The phrase probably refers to the widespread desire of Jewish women to give birth to the Messiah. Therefore, it isn't his lack of desire for women, but rather his contempt for their desire for the Messiah to come. "What this passage accordingly predicted was that he, as a Gentile, will have a total disregard for Scripture and its promise of a coming King of kings." Walvoord, *The Prophecy Knowledge Handbook*, 272. Also see Campbell, *Daniel*, 171; and Pentecost, "Daniel," 1371.

15. Many have speculated about the identity of these kingdoms. The temptation in interpreting this section of prophecy is to allow current events to inform the Scripture rather than the other way around. In this Bible Companion, we've chosen to remain silent about the

specific identities of these kingdoms, as well as the reference in 11:44 to the "East," unless a nation is specifically identified by name in Scripture (as Libya, Ethiopia, and Egypt are in 11:43). Any other identification we might make would be pure conjecture.

16. Mysteriously, Edom, Moab, and Ammon (presently included in the kingdom of Jordan) will escape the Antichrist's conquest during his war with the kingdoms of the South and North (Daniel 11:41).

17. The phrase "your people" makes it clear that Gabriel was speaking about the Jews in this immediate context. But as we'll see in lesson 8, and especially as we look at the parallel passage of Revelation 20:12 and 15, those "found written in the book" (Daniel 12:1) will include Gentiles as well.

18. John F. Kennedy, "Address Before the General Assembly of the United Nations" (September 25, 1961), in *Let the Word Go Forth: The Speeches, Statements, and Writings of John F. Kennedy, 1943–1963*, ed. Theodore C. Sorensen (New York: Delacorte Press, 1988), 378.

LESSON EIGHT

1. H. L. Mencken, *Minority Report: H. L. Mencken's Notebooks* (New York: Knopf, 1956), 234.

2. Alexander Hamilton, "72: Re-eligibility of the President," in *The Federalist*, ed. Benjamin F. Wright (New York: Barnes & Noble Books, 1996), 464.

3. See for example Exodus 32:33; Isaiah 34:16; Malachi 3:16; Luke 10:20; Philippians 4:3; Revelation 3:5; 13:8; 17:8; 20:12, 15; 21:27, 22.19.

4. During His ministry, Jesus raised Lazarus (John 11), Jairus's daughter (Mark 5:35–43; Luke 8:47–56), and others (Luke 7:11–17) from the dead. But these restorations from the dead are not included in the four general resurrections studied in this chapter for a couple of reasons. First, these people had just died when Jesus brought

them back—not to their eternal, renewed bodies but to their *earthly* bodies. At God's appointed time, each one died again. Second, these resurrections were specific miracles completed for the purpose of pointing to Jesus as the Messiah. On the other hand, the four general resurrections have a very different purpose. They will bring every person to the place where he or she will spend eternity, based upon each person's relationship with Jesus Christ.

5. Old Testament saints were saved by grace through faith in God, as Paul made clear in Romans 4:16–25.

6. Walter Bauer and others, *A Greek-English Lexicon of the New Testament and other Early Christian Literature*, 3d. ed., rev. and ed. Frederick William Danker (Chicago: University of Chicago, 2000), 943–44.

7. Albert Camus, quoted in Olivier Todd, *Albert Camus: A Life*, trans. Benjamin Ivry (New York: Knopf, 1999), 212.

LESSON NINE

1. Stephen W. Hawking, *A Brief History of Time: From the Big Bang to Black Holes* (New York: Bantam Books, 1988), 175.

2. For more information, see John A. Witmer, "Jesus Christ: Knowing Jesus as Man and God," in *Understanding Christian Theology*, ed. Charles R. Swindoll and Roy B. Zuck (Nashville: Thomas Nelson, 2003), 300–5.

3. J. Dwight Pentecost, "Daniel," in *The Bible Knowledge Commentary: Old Testament*, ed. John F. Walvoord and Roy B. Zuck (Wheaton, Ill.: Victor Books, 1986), 1366. See also lesson 6, "Supernatural Phenomena between Heaven and Earth," note 4.

4. "Time" equals one year, "times" two years, and "half a time" six months. This corresponds to the 1,260 days of the great tribulation described in Revelation 12:6 and the forty-two months in Revelation 11:2; 13:5. This period of time was established in Daniel's earlier visions (Daniel 7:25; 9:27).

5. See Donald K. Campbell, *Daniel: God's Man in a Secular Society* (Grand Rapids: Discovery House, 1988), 183–84; and John F. Walvoord, *The Prophecy Knowledge Handbook* (Wheaton, Ill.: SP Publications, 1990), 278. It should be noted that theologians have offered at least two other possibilities to account for these thirty days. First, because the terrible battle of Armageddon will be such a bloody affair, it might take time to clean it up in preparation for the millennial kingdom, even with the presence of the carrion birds (Revelation 19:17–21). Second, the Antichrist may announce the abolishment of the sacrifice and his intention to establish an idol in the temple thirty days before the actual commencement of these events (which mark the beginning of the 1,260-day great tribulation). See Pentecost, "Daniel," 1374.

6. See Campbell, *Daniel*, 184.

7. Daniel, along with the other Old Testament saints—who were saved by grace through faith as they followed the old covenant—will be resurrected to "everlasting life" at the second coming of Christ (Daniel 12:2; Isaiah 26:19). For more information, see John F. Walvoord, "End Times: Understanding Today's World Events in Biblical Prophecy," in *Understanding Christian Theology*, ed. Charles R. Swindoll and Roy B. Zuck (Nashville: Thomas Nelson, 2003), 1336–37.

8. Benjamin Franklin, *Poor Richard's Almanack* (New York: Barnes and Noble Books, 2004), 292.

9. Blaise Pascal, *Pensées*, 188, trans. A. J. Krailsheimer (New York: Penguin Books, 1995), 56.

The crossword puzzle answer key.

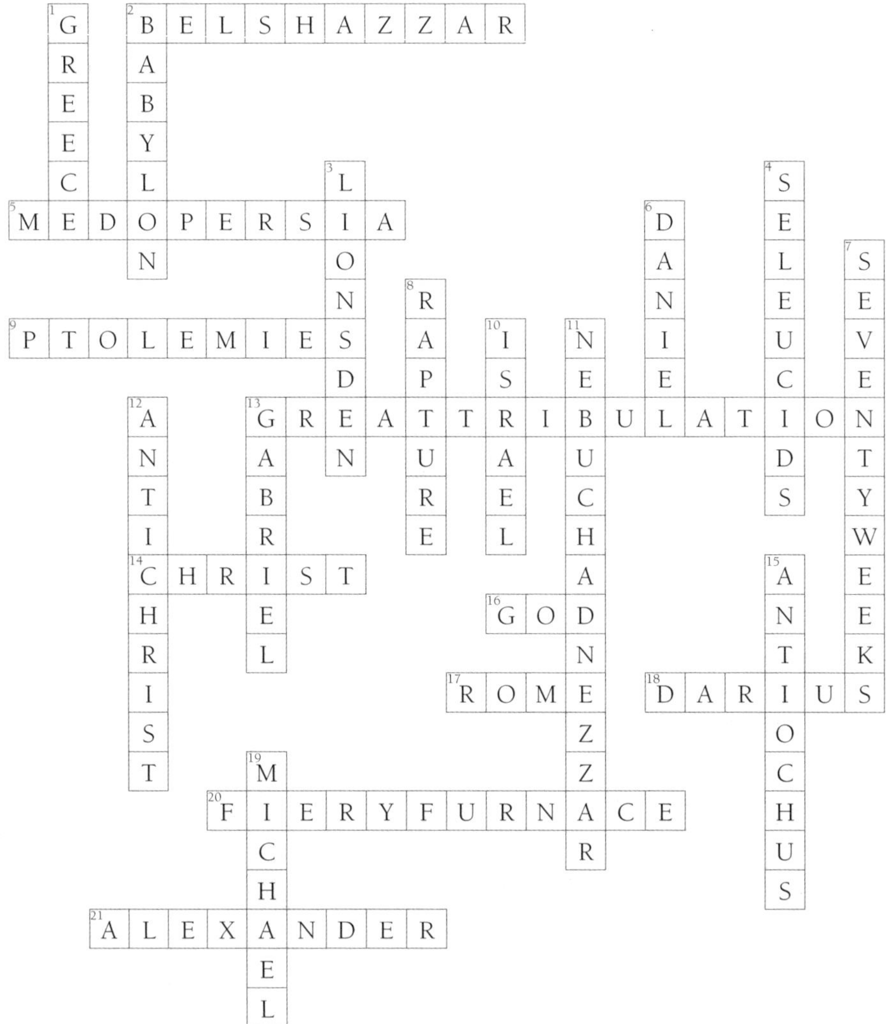

RESOURCES FOR PROBING FURTHER

Daniel confessed that he didn't understand the visions and prophecies given to him (Daniel 12:8). No doubt they are difficult to grasp, but after working your way through *Daniel, Volume 2: God's Plan for the Future Bible Companion*, you should now have a better understanding of some of the most enigmatic prophecies in Scripture. Your knowledge of the prophecies in the book of Daniel will also help you unlock the meaning of other prophecies, particularly those contained in the other great prophetic book, Revelation.

So to further your study of the book of Daniel and prophecy in general, we recommend the following resources. Of course, we cannot always endorse everything a writer or ministry says, so we encourage you to approach these and all other non-biblical resources with wisdom and discernment.

Campbell, Donald K. *Daniel: God's Man in a Secular Society*. Grand Rapids: Discovery House, 1988.

Insight for Living. *Daniel, Volume 1: God's Man for the Moment Bible Companion*. Plano, Tex.: IFL Publishing House, 2008.

Insight for Living. *Revelation—Unveiling the End, Act 1: The Heavenly Stage*. Plano, Tex.: IFL Publishing House, 2006.

Insight for Living. *Revelation—Unveiling the End, Act 2: The Earthly Drama*. Plano, Tex.: IFL Publishing House, 2006.

Insight for Living. *Revelation—Unveiling the End, Act 3: The Final Curtain*. Plano, Tex.: IFL Publishing House, 2007.

Jeremiah, David, with C. C. Carlson. *The Handwriting on the Wall: Secrets from the Prophecies of Daniel*. Nashville: W Publishing, 1992.

Pentecost, J. Dwight. "Daniel." In *The Bible Knowledge Commentary: Old Testament*, 1323-75. Ed. John F. Walvoord and Roy B. Zuck. Wheaton, Ill.: Victor Books, 1986.

Swindoll, Charles R., and Roy B. Zuck, eds. *Understanding Christian Theology*. Nashville: Thomas Nelson, 2003.

Wallace, Ronald S. *The Message of Daniel*. The Bible Speaks Today series. Downers Grove, Ill.: InterVarsity, 1984.

Walvoord, John F. *End Times: Understanding Today's World Events in Biblical Prophecy*. Nashville: Word, 1998.

Walvoord, John F. *The Prophecy Knowledge Handbook*. Wheaton, Ill.: SP Publications, 1990.

Wiersbe, Warren W. *The Wiersbe Bible Commentary: The Complete Old Testament in One Volume*. Colorado Springs: David C. Cook, 2007.

ORDERING INFORMATION

If you would like to order additional copies of *Daniel, Volume 2: God's Plan for the Future Bible Companion* or order other Insight for Living resources, please contact the office that serves you.

United States

Insight for Living
Post Office Box 269000
Plano, Texas 75026-9000
USA
1-800-772-8888
(Monday through Thursday
7:00 a.m. – 9:00 p.m. and
Friday 7:00 a.m. – 7:00 p.m.
Central time)
www.insight.org
www.insightworld.org

Canada

Insight for Living Canada
Post Office Box 2510
Vancouver, BC V6B 3W7
CANADA
1-800-663-7639
www.insightforliving.ca

Australia, New Zealand, and South Pacific

Insight for Living Australia
Post Office Box 1011
Bayswater, VIC 3153
AUSTRALIA
1300 467 444
www.insight.asn.au

United Kingdom and Europe

Insight for Living United Kingdom
Post Office Box 348
Leatherhead
KT22 2DS
UNITED KINGDOM
0800 915 9364
www.insightforliving.org.uk

Other International Locations

International constituents may contact the U.S. office through our Web site (www.insightworld.org), mail queries, or by calling +1-972-473-5136.

NOTES

NOTES